CW00706378

THE MAN WHO NEVER HEARD 'NO'
AND CREATED SOMETHING GREAT

RICHARD EMERSON

═══ THE HOPFATHER ═══

BY MICHAEL DONALDSON

PENGUIN BOOKS

PENGUIN

UK | USA | Canada | Ireland | Australia
India | New Zealand | South Africa | China

Penguin is an imprint of the Penguin Random House group of companies, whose addresses can be
found at global.penguinrandomhouse.com.

First published by Penguin Random House New Zealand, 2019

10 9 8 7 6 5 4 3 2 1

Text © The Emerson Brewing Company, 2019
Photographs © Emerson collection, unless otherwise credited
Cover photograph © Derek Morrison, Adventure Media Group

The moral right of Michael Donaldson to be identified as the author has been asserted.

All rights reserved. Without limiting the rights under copyright reserved above, no part of this
publication may be reproduced, stored in or introduced into a retrieval system, or transmitted, in any
form or by any means (electronic, mechanical, photocopying, recording or otherwise), without the prior
written permission of both the copyright owner and the above publisher of this book.

Design by Gary Stewart © Penguin Random House New Zealand
Prepress by Image Centre Group
Printed and bound in China by RR Donnelley

A catalogue record for this book is available from the National Library of New Zealand.

ISBN 978-0-14-377367-2
eISBN 978-0-14-377368-9

penguin.co.nz

CONTENTS

PROLOGUE

On 7 November 2012, Richard Emerson woke up a millionaire.

The previous day, Emerson's Brewery officially sold to New Zealand brewing giant Lion for a sum of $8 million. Richard's 12.1 per cent share in the business that carried his name netted him close to $1 million. That wasn't all though — his mother Ingrid received a cheque for double that amount, half of which was to be held in trust for Richard as a form of early inheritance.

This was the kind of instant wealth people dream about when they buy a Lotto ticket. Except this wealth wasn't instant, nor did it just happen overnight. For Richard, it came after 20 years of unrelenting commitment to the cause of good beer. They were two decades of hard graft, physically and emotionally, of little or no pay, and of long hours, during which he watched his father, mentor and friend die just as the business began to stand on its own two feet. During that time, he'd dealt with a broken marriage and the never-ending stress of making ends meet while trying to grow a business in a market that had little or no understanding of good beer.

For Ingrid Emerson, the payout was a reward not just for the 20-year investment she and her husband George had made in their son's business, but also for the almost 50-year investment she'd made in Richard — in teaching him the skills he needed to find his place in the world. It was a reward for the love and dedication she'd given to ensuring her profoundly deaf son wouldn't just get by, but would also find success in a world where he would always struggle to fully understand other people, a world where he often felt isolated, different and misunderstood.

But it was never about money — for either of them. Richard shrugs at the idea of being a self-made millionaire. 'It's nice to have something in your back pocket,' he says with a smile.

Ingrid takes her fulfilment from the fact that Richard triumphed against all odds, and that she prevailed when others questioned what the hell she was doing as she tenaciously fought to guarantee her son would never be held back by his disability.

Theirs is a story not of tough love, but of practical love, of single-minded determination — from Ingrid, George and Richard. It's a story about the power of a family. And it's a reminder that a slow train ride is just as enjoyable as the fast-track to success.

This is the story of an adventurous boy who wouldn't let anything get in the way of what he wanted to do; a boy who fought for his place in the world and refused to let anyone tell him 'no'.

Richard has a lifelong love of trains, inherited from his father's love of railway photography.

YOU KNOW HE'S DEAF, DON'T YOU?

As a very young child, I was aware of thumps on the ground and loud noises. I would look around to see what it was and where it had come from. It took so long for me to hear that I was behind in terms of learning to read. My mother put in a lot of effort to help me learn to lip-read. She would have a spoon in her hand and hold it up to her face and say 'spoon'. It wasn't easy for my mother, especially when I couldn't say the word 'Mum'. I would call her 'Bum'.

A young Richard Emerson with an early set of hearing aids. Richard was so profoundly deaf he had hearing aids in both ears rather than one as was more common in the late 1960s.

Looking back, Ingrid Emerson wonders what she would do given a choice. Go through with her pregnancy knowing her first-born child would more than likely suffer a severe birth defect? Or, as others did later, terminate the pregnancy?

'What would I do if I had my time over? If I knew I had rubella would I have an abortion or not? I still don't know. Back then we had no choice but to take the risk.'

. . .

Ingrid Holst married George Emerson in 1958, and they lived in a small flat near the University of Otago in Dunedin. Having gained a Bachelor of Science degree, she worked in the university's biochemistry department where George was studying towards his PhD.

Ingrid knew she had married a scientist with a train obsession and a camera, a man with a passion for documenting railway infrastructure and the end of the steam age. Perhaps not quite as obvious was that she'd married a man with an Elizabethan approach to married life — what George wanted he got.

In October 1963, George wanted to spend Labour Weekend in Christchurch to indulge his passion for photographing steam trains. Ingrid dutifully packed the Commer Cob on which they'd recently spent their meagre savings, and off they went. The Commer was a cross between a station wagon and a van, and they'd bought it so they could save money by sleeping in it on George's frequent train-chasing weekends away.

Ingrid, who was a few weeks pregnant at the time, can't remember the specific reason for the trip as there were so many train-related holidays over the years, she reckons they've all blurred into one.

The one detail of the trip she remembers clearly wasn't to make itself known until a couple of weeks after they got home. 'I noticed when I had a bath I had a rash all over me. I went to the GP the next morning and he happened to have a skin specialist in his suite of rooms. They looked at it and decided it was rubella.

'I had to go to the health department to get gamma-globulin — I don't know what good it did you, but that was the only treatment they could give you . . . that or an abortion, but an abortion wasn't mentioned at that moment at all. They did after that — in fact, women demanded it — when the next bout of rubella came around.

'After Richard was born, a lot of people said to me: "I had an abortion, why didn't you?" Medical people asked me the same question when Richard was a little boy. One person said: "What do you feel about having Richard like this?" I remember saying it's a hang of a lot of work, but I wouldn't be without him. Because what a fabulous addition to the world he's been, what a lot he's done for people, what a lot he's done for Dunedin.

'Off and on in those early years I did wonder, especially when these younger women were having abortions, did they know what they were doing?'

For such a mild disease for those infected, rubella's danger for unborn children seems disproportionate.

As Ingrid discovered in the bath, rubella — or German measles — is characterised by a rash with little or no fever. Caused by an airborne virus, rubella's symptoms are often so mild that around half of those who are infected are unaware they even have it.

As academics, George and Ingrid had access to research on rubella, much of which had been driven by Australian paediatric ophthalmologist Norman Gregg, who first made the link between the disease and pregnancy in 1942 as a result of a high incidence of congenital cataracts in infants arriving at his surgery. When he overheard a group of mothers discussing the fact they had all contracted German measles during pregnancy he made the connection.

Ingrid and George knew their unborn child may not reach full-term, as miscarriages were common in pregnant women who contracted the disease. They also had to contend with the possibility that their child could be stillborn. If the child survived, they faced the possibility of having a disability such as deafness, cataracts, a heart disorder, developmental delays or autism.

The only treatment available to Ingrid was the gamma-globulin injections, which were given to try to temporarily boost both her and her unborn child's immunity against the disease. After that, the expectant parents spent nine months in limbo, uncertain of their child's fate. 'We knew what the risks were, but all we could do was hope.'

. . .

Richard George Emerson came into the world on 17 June 1964, with Ingrid and George braced for bad news as their newborn was taken away to be examined.

'Our family doctor delivered him and he said, "He looks fine, his heart's fine, it looks like his eyes are okay,"' Ingrid recalled. 'As a newborn he was so lively, his eyes darted around after every movement and he had a bright smile. He did all the right things.'

Ingrid and George counted their blessings; Richard had a greater than 50 per cent chance of having some kind of disability, but he appeared happy and healthy. The possibility of a hearing problem remained as around 58 per cent of children whose mothers have been infected with rubella turn out to be profoundly deaf, but they wouldn't know for certain for another six months. At that age, children usually start to turn their heads in response to sound.

When Richard was about six months old, Ingrid arranged to see another young mother, with whom she'd been in the Queen Mary Maternity Hospital. 'We met in town for a coffee, with our babies in their pushchairs. I noticed immediately that her baby boy — who was the same age as Richard — sounded completely different to my boy. Hers was going "ga-ga-ga, da-da-da" and mine was going "aaahhh-aaahhh-ah". I realised Richard wasn't making any consonants.'

As a result of this meeting, a visit from a Plunket nurse was hastily arranged. She gave Richard a range of tests related to his hearing. One included rustling paper behind the baby's back to see if he reacted. Ingrid told the nurse to be extra careful not to let Richard see the paper because his curious eyes would follow it. Nothing escaped his vigilance. Little wonder then that the test showed he relied on his eyes for his information about the world because he had a serious hearing problem. Further tests revealed that Richard was profoundly deaf. He couldn't hear anything below 90 decibels, or the noise level of your average lawn mower.

Once his deafness had been established, Richard was fitted with his first hearing aids at the age of nine months. At that age, most deaf children were given a single hearing aid, but the severity of Richard's hearing loss pushed Dunedin audiologist Alec Mair to prescribe two.

Richard wore the bulky hearing aid receivers in a harness on his chest with wires connecting to an earpiece where the sound was broadcast. With their help, he could now pick up directional sound.

The hearing aids weren't going to be enough on their own, so Ingrid decided she would help Richard learn to communicate. She decided on lip-reading because, while sign language existed in New Zealand in the 1960s, it was discouraged by educators and had been completely banned in deaf schools throughout the country, something that didn't change until the late 1970s. As a result, much of the language developed in secret or across small communities without any consistency across the country. There was no coherent system in place until the late 1990s and it wasn't until 2006 that New Zealand sign became an official language of this country.

For Ingrid, teaching lip-reading had more practical roots. 'There was no way I was going to learn sign language just for Richard to learn it,' she said in her forthright, pragmatic manner. 'I'd have to teach it to everyone who visited, to grandparents, to friends . . . it just didn't make sense at all.

WHILE SIGN LANGUAGE EXISTED IN NEW ZEALAND IN THE 1960S, IT WAS DISCOURAGED BY EDUCATORS AND HAD BEEN COMPLETELY BANNED IN DEAF SCHOOLS THROUGHOUT THE COUNTRY.

We had this idea Richard was the only deaf person we were ever likely to meet and we had to work out how we would introduce him to our world. We were determined he had to fit into our world — we weren't going to fit into a deaf world.'

Ingrid faced months of demanding and exasperating work to have Richard understand her intention let alone the words. She would sit him in his highchair and wait until he made eye contact, which took a long time because of Richard's propensity for playing, fiddling and looking around the room. Once she had his attention, she would hold up an object and say its name: 'ball' or 'spoon'.

She had help from Jocelyn Ward, an advisor to parents of deaf children, who toured the Otago region. Ingrid saw her once a fortnight. Ward played a vital part in Ingrid's own education as she learned from scratch the methods required to teach her son. Ward advised Ingrid and George to visit the Sumner School for the Deaf — now van Asch Deaf Education Centre — in Christchurch to see a very good teacher in action. 'We hoped to never send him to the School for the Deaf in Sumner,' Ingrid said. 'But Jocelyn said we should go there to see this teacher.'

Richard was three when the family packed up the Commer Cob to head north. Before they left, George realised that making the young boy sit in the back seat with nothing but a view of the seat in front of him would rob him of his main connection to the world. To make the trip more interesting for Richard, George built a raised seat from canvas and tent poles that hooked over the back seat and allowed his son to sit up high enough to see the world as it passed by. The jury-rigged child seat wouldn't meet modern standards, but at the time it was a case of needs-must for a headstrong boy who struggled to understand unless he could see.

When they got to Christchurch, the family sat in on a class at the School for the Deaf and focused on the teacher. As Ingrid remembers, the teacher didn't speak until she got the children's attention — and when she did speak, she avoided the one-word-at-a-time approach Ingrid had employed with Richard. Instead she spoke a phrase in a normal tone. 'This is a ball.' 'This is a blue ball.'

The value of speaking with a natural emphasis and tone turned on a light for Ingrid. Teaching Richard words in isolation didn't help him as that wasn't how people spoke.

After the class, the teacher told Ingrid that all of the children in her care would lip-read well enough to enter mainstream schools at the age of five.

Ingrid left Christchurch set in her belief that Richard would do the same; he would be ready for mainstream education even if she had to do all the groundwork herself. And she would have to.

She was alone, almost isolated, as the mother of a deaf child in Dunedin, whereas in Christchurch, the rubella epidemic had created a cohort of deaf children all around the same age as Richard. The way rubella spread, it hadn't reached Dunedin until six or seven months after Ingrid had contracted it in Christchurch. That made Richard an outlier, at least seven months older than the group of children affected by rubella in the Dunedin wave. 'That was just the way the rubella epidemic spread through New Zealand,' Ingrid said, 'so we were ahead of the group, which was a little bit awkward.'

Her resolve to proceed alone was based largely on the fact that Richard was out on a limb in terms of support services. Looking back, she believes other parents of deaf children — perhaps because they were part of a larger group — were happy to sit back and wait for solutions to arrive. 'People would say to me, "Oh, you spend so much time with him." Well, what else

was I going to do? How was he expected to learn? Others seemed to be waiting for the education system to do something for their kids — well, all those hours you've wasted waiting for something that might not happen, and every wonderful opportunity when the child wanted to know something and you palmed them off or didn't want to delve into it.

'And we thought he was going to be our only child, so we could afford to put the time and effort in.'

Ingrid was relentless. 'Bloody-minded' is a word used to describe her by family. It is a trait Richard has also inherited, which made some of their sessions together quite a trial. Ingrid bought an AmpliVox, a device that allowed her to speak into a microphone, which sent the amplified sound to a set of headphones worn by Richard. It allowed for more focused learning as it cut out background noise that would be picked up by his hearing aids. As a result, Richard was less distracted and could focus more directly on his mother.

Ingrid quickly realised her son was clever. While rubella in utero can cause a range of learning disabilities, Richard was bright and engaged — but he was also hyper-energetic and single-mindedly inquisitive. Keeping

If Richard did not know the name of an object he would point to it in a picture book and his mother, Ingrid, would say it so he could lip-read the name.

Richard was an adventurous child who refused to let his deafness stop him from enjoying life.

him still for any length of time proved impossible and many lessons were taught on the run as Ingrid followed him around the house. A picture from a family album that shows her in pursuit of her wee blond boy was not atypical. Lessons would happen in cupboards, in the garden, sitting on the floor, going up and down stairs. '"Up" was an easy word for him to say, "down" was much harder.'

Later in 1967, the Emersons bought their first house, a villa in Maori Hill where Ingrid still lives. It was handy to the university, it had a north-facing backyard and it was strategically situated on a quiet one-way street, making it ideal for a tearaway deaf boy.

Richard never let his deafness slow him down. In many ways it had the opposite effect, by increasing his desire to see and understand the world around him. From a very young age, he had an eye for adventure and a nose for trouble, and he was always on high alert for opportunities to play.

Ingrid used to take him to her regular meetings at the YWCA. There, she and other young mothers would have coffee and listen to guest speakers as their children played nearby. One day, Ingrid had barely sat down with her coffee when another mother came up to her saying: 'Your little boy is running up the road, I called out but he wouldn't come back.'

'You know he's deaf, don't you?' said Ingrid, as she got to her feet and set off in pursuit of her son.

The frustration in learning to lip-read is that there are so many words in the English language that look all the same to me. That was the case with 'mum' and 'bum'. When lip-reading, the M and the B, and sometimes P, come out identical. The hearing person can hear the difference as the M is heard with more 'Mmmm' vibration, while B and P are slightly shorter and a little more explosive. However, those differences are far too subtle to pick up in lip-reading, so I have to resort to working out what the word is by how it is used in the context of the sentence. Unfortunately, the context can be just as bad! For example, 'Have you seen my mum?' can be 'Have you seen my bum?' or 'Where is my puppy?' instead of 'Where is my mummy?'

Mum and Dad always took pains to look at me to try to explain the words, what they meant and how they are used in context. But, faark, there were many occasions where the words never could sound right because those so-called English words were taken from other languages and pronounced differently to the way they looked!

Mum tells me she used to hold items beside her face and make sure that I was looking at her face when she tried to mouth the words clearly. It took a while, but I finally learned to accept that her lip movements meant what the item was.

Lip-reading can be quite relaxing or it can be bloody hard — when I meet people for the first time it can be quite a defining moment. I can either read people instantly or it takes a lot of work to understand the different movements of their lips, their accents, the way they talk.

Some of the worst people are the ones with the stiff upper lip — literally, people with a stiff upper lip means I have to work really hard to understand them. Other people, when I get to know them well, I can lip-read them from the side of the face. But everyone has to face me to be fully understood. Even at primary school I had to get my friends to look at me. They got to know this is what they had to do. They used to wave to get my attention and sometimes they used to whistle — I can hear those kinds of sounds.

It took a long time for Ingrid to teach Richard the correct pronunciation of 'Mum' — months were spent putting up with Richard calling out 'Bum!' in public when he wanted her attention. Through trial and error, she was able to teach him that 'Mum' comes with a vibration that Richard could feel by pressing his finger against the side of his nose.

There were other subtleties that took time to perfect. For instance, Ingrid would hold up a feather and accent the F sound by blowing on it. The difference between K and hard G sounds was also difficult, meaning pink could be pig for Richard.

As Ingrid taught Richard to read and write to ready him for school, he did so left-handed. At one stage Ingrid's mother-in-law, who had been a schoolteacher, noted Richard had a preference for his left hand, and she told Ingrid, 'You'll have to change that — you have to insist he uses his right hand.' To which Ingrid replied, 'He's got such a problem with his hearing to deal with I don't need to muddle him up further.'

New words were learned from Richard Scarry's highly illustrated books *Best Word Book Ever*, *Storybook Dictionary* and *What Do People Do All Day?* Ingrid has kept these battered and torn books for over half a century. When Richard didn't know the word for something, he would search out the picture of it in these books and Ingrid would pronounce it for him.

Part of the reason Ingrid succeeded in teaching her son to lip-read was her own dogged determination — she understood that if she didn't do it herself, no one else was going to volunteer. She and George were also focused on the end goal: that Richard would fit into the world, not be separate from it.

They put so much effort into Richard, they worried he might start to believe the world revolved around him. Ingrid didn't take long to realise her son 'didn't know the meaning of "no". Everything he wanted he got.' It was an attitude that would serve him well in later life as he built his business, but as a young boy it was a trait that was unlikely to win him any friends. From then on, the couple decided that Richard needed to learn that his peers weren't going to go out of their way for him just because he had a disability.

'I started him at Playcentre early because I felt he needed to be with other children. He needed to realise that other children would grab things off you and fight with you. He had the potential to be isolated, but I wanted him to interact and socialise. It was hard on him. I can remember many times bringing him home in tears and he would often come to me crying, holding his hands over his ears because he was unable to handle the high-pitched screaming of other children, which was amplified by his hearing aids.'

While Ingrid was busy teaching Richard at home, George engaged with the broader deaf community in Dunedin. Richard's audiologist, Alec Mair, had been instrumental in establishing the Otago Deaf Society, and by 1967, George was on the group's organising committee. This put the family in touch with other deaf people in Dunedin and helped them to understand the challenges Richard would face.

. . .

When he turned five in the middle of 1969, Richard was on his own — the only deaf child in his class at Maori Hill School. Pictures of Richard from those years show a bright, handsome boy with the blondest hair and the bluest eyes. His smile is electric. He was an intelligent child who made rapid progress. Ingrid recalls one of his early teachers saying she'd never met a child like Richard before. She was so captivated by his charm and energy that she moved to Christchurch to learn to become a teacher for the deaf.

There was a group of deaf children scheduled to start school the following year — many of whom were affected by rubella — and their parents were working towards creating a unit that would cater for deaf children at Arthur Street School. The unit's establishment was being driven by the Otago Deaf Society, with George Emerson on the committee.

Despite their involvement with the Deaf Society, both George and Ingrid

George Emerson's passion was trains — and railway infrastructure such as platforms, tunnels and bridges — and they became an integral part of Richard's life from an early age.

retained their belief in the need to push Richard out into the world. They pushed for him to start school in a mainstream classroom rather than wait for six months for the other deaf children in the area to reach school age.

Whether through a misunderstanding or a miscommunication, the staff at Maori Hill School thought that Richard would only be there until the end of 1969 and he would then move to the soon-to-be-opened deaf unit.

With help from Jocelyn Ward and a local education inspector, Ingrid decided that Richard had done so well in the mainstream environment and was so well settled that he should keep going to Maori Hill School. Their decision elicited a visit from the school's headmaster, who demanded to know why Richard would not be attending the deaf unit: 'Your group has fought for so long to get that class — why are you not going to it?'

Ingrid stood staunchly by her decision. She was convinced Richard could cope with mainstream schooling; that it was good for both his education and personal development. She became more convinced she was on the right track when she offered to volunteer at the deaf unit during its first year. She tried some of the same teaching methods she'd used with Richard, but found it much harder to connect with this group of children — even though many had the same kind of disability as her son.

Whether it was a mother's bias or just familiarity with her own son, she believed he was ahead of the group in terms of learning and socialisation. 'Richard would not have liked that class at all; I felt it would have been a waste of time for him.'

Ingrid and George strived to keep their son out of his comfort zone and to challenge him, and they didn't wait for help to arrive. They were assisted by the fact Richard had a personality that matched their demands.

A lasting memory for Ingrid that demonstrated Richard's personality — his sense of adventure, love of food and sheer determination — was his propensity for biscuit-stealing. He was notorious for raiding his mother's baking tins for late-night snacks. It was not unusual to find him asleep surrounded by biscuit crumbs. The answer, she thought, was to put the biscuit tin high up in the pantry. All it did was encourage Richard to take the challenge of climbing the pantry shelves like a young Edmund Hillary to reach his goal.

The next step was to put a chain and padlock around the cupboard doors. But Richard saw there was a bit of slack in the chain and he could get the cupboard open just enough to wedge his hand through and get a biscuit,

plucked one at a time between two fingers working like chopsticks. 'I pulled them out one by one and shut the door quietly. Mum was mystified the biscuits could disappear despite the door being locked. Mum's answer was to give up making biscuits for a while.'

· · ·

After Richard's deafness was diagnosed, Ingrid and George threw all their energy into him — and for a long time they thought he would be their only child.

Richard grew up thinking one of the reasons he didn't have any siblings until he was seven was due to the fact he was such a handful his parents wouldn't cope with another child; that they put off having more children because of him. The truth is a little more harrowing.

'I had three miscarriages between Richard and Helen,' Ingrid said. 'They were all a bit disastrous. One was when he was about 18 months old. After I lost that baby, there was a little piece in the paper — I wished I'd kept it — saying doctors weren't doing operations on cataracts in children who'd been exposed to rubella in utero as they were finding live rubella virus.'

According to medical literature, once a woman has recovered from

Richard with his paternal grandparents Albert and Dorothy Emerson.

rubella it should not affect future pregnancies, but that story about the virus continuing to live on in exposed children gave Ingrid pause for thought. She believed the virus somehow continued to impact on her ability to carry a pregnancy to full term. 'I've never researched that — but I'm presuming that's why I lost them.'

The birth of Richard's younger sister Helen, when he was seven, was one of the most important events in his young life. He'd been envious of the family next door who had a boy a little older than Richard and a younger daughter. Richard saw this as a model family and thought the Emerson household was incomplete without a younger sister.

'After waiting a long time, Helen came. And Richard thought it was delightful that we were a complete family. That's what he said: "Now we're a family."'

Opposite: Ingrid and Richard on an outing with other children from the Otago Deaf Society.
Above: Richard was delighted when his baby sister Helen was born.

THE RIDE OF
A LIFETIME

I've always loved trains. When I was boy in the late 1960s, steam trains were still around, but they were on their way out. My father was very eager to get out and record these disappearing trains.

For me, it was a wonderful experience. I was exposed to the very loud 'chuff, chuff, chuff' of the engine — it was a visual pleasure, as well as visceral and loud. I really enjoyed the click and clack of the rails, the movement of the carriages, the smell of the steam and coal. And I could feel the heat.

Richard loved steam engines for their noise, their smell and the vibration they made.

The train driver was the hero for me. He was in charge, and when I was young all I wanted to be was a train driver. But I was born too late. By the time I was old enough to drive a train they were all controlled by radio telephones. I would have made a terrible job of it.

Dad loved trains, but more from the perspective of a railway archaeologist, a pictorialist. He liked the steam trains in action, but he also wanted to record a snapshot in time when the railway infrastructure was going and a way of life was disappearing. He was specifically interested in the area around Central Otago. He was a railway historian — taking photos of things other people took for granted and might not notice when they are gone.

My mother was a railway widow, sitting in the car doing her knitting while Dad and I were running across the country looking for steam trains. Bill Cowan, who wrote a couple of books on steam trains, told me that my father wasn't like a lot of other photographers who would park on the road next to the track, get a quick photo and move on. Dad would go further — he would walk to the hard-to-reach places and get the better photographs. We'd sometimes walk and wait three or four hours for a photograph.

My father travelled the country looking for trains, and it was a good experience for me to learn places and geography.

Ingrid, Richard and George.

George West Emerson was a driving force in Richard's life. While he didn't give his son a love of beer — Richard found that on his own — George did pass on his passion for trains, imbuing Richard with a lifelong love of all things rail, particularly steam trains.

Like any father and son, George and Richard Emerson clashed — both strong-willed, stubborn and determined to do things their own way — and yet they shared many common interests, so much so that Richard came to see his dad as his best mate.

George, however, was not always easy to love. Even those closest to George describe him as a curmudgeon, stern, grumpy, a bully, even Elizabethan in the sense he controlled the finances and made all the family decisions. In an interview late in life, George admitted while not quite 'the Ayatollah' he recognised the 'dictator' in himself.

Ingrid Emerson says her first encounter with her future husband left her thinking 'he was the rudest man I'd ever met'.

Helen Emerson, Richard's younger sister, says her father was frugal, firm, fastidious but always fair. 'He was no-frills, puritanical, but we had all the essentials and it was a very caring, loving home.'

Richard, pictured with his father George, used to record steam trains on a cassette recorder so he could replay the sound later on.

George drove everything in the family's life and what George said went. Fiscally conservative, he hated spending money and would never pay for someone to do something he might be able to do himself.

George decided when and where the family would holiday, a schedule usually built around trains. Helen recalls a tedious — for her — Easter Weekend spent in a motel in the unglamorous Southland town of Lumsden; the Emerson family and other train enthusiasts booking out the entire place so George, Richard and others could chase the Kingston Flyer.

The family joke has Richard chasing his first train while sitting on a potty — and even that was at the mercy of George's control. On one of the many family trips spent indulging George's obsession for train photography, Richard's need to relieve himself coincided with George's need to get in the car and drive to the next train-snapping spot, so off they went in the car with Ingrid balancing Richard on a portable potty. As Richard says with a smile, 'George was so impatient he wasn't letting my shit get in the way of photographing a steam train.'

Meanwhile, at home the radio stayed tuned to the station George wanted to listen to and silence reigned when the news came on. The Bakelite radio was so old, however, it had to be turned on well in advance of any news bulletin as it needed time to warm up; but it worked and therefore didn't need to be replaced or updated.

Equally aged was the family's worn-out Triumph 2000 car. It so embarrassed Helen when George drove her to school, she demanded that he park on a side road short of the main gate. She didn't want any of her friends to see the car, but George ignored her embarrassed pleas and drove right to the gate. 'He knew damn well what he was doing — he was driving all the way to the school gate whether I wanted him to or not!'

George had high expectations of himself and of Richard and Helen. Did he demand more of Richard because of his disability than he would have done with a mythical son who doesn't exist? Probably not, say family members.

Richard's disability cut him no favours, but nor did George over-discipline his son. On the contrary, one of Richard's long-time friends remembers George 'driving' Richard to ensure his disability didn't hold him back, didn't make him a victim and didn't give him a handy excuse for not achieving his full potential.

As a child, I was afraid of my father. My friends were afraid of him. Often when I got into trouble it took me a long time to work out why he would discipline me. Other times it was more obvious.

One snowy day when I was walking home from school at lunchtime, my friend Rob Smillie said to me, 'I dare you to throw a snowball at a car.' So I did. The snowball hit the car, but it turned out the snowball had a stone in it and it chipped the windscreen of the car. Sheeeit! I was off running as fast as I could home.

The man in the car caught up with Rob and demanded to know where I lived. Rob was a bit of a stirrer and he wanted to see what would happen next, so he pointed to our house.

Dad was in bed with the flu, the doorbell rang, my mother answered and there was this man in a long trench coat. He outlined for her what I had done.

The next thing I saw was my father getting out of bed . . . Faaark, I knew what this meant — I was in for a hiding! I was so terrified that I rushed out the front door and ran down the street. Dad finally grabbed me and dragged me home into the hallway. Then he picked up a piece of wood that was lying around from some renovation work and whacked me. Oh boy, I bawled my eyes out and he made me go back to school red-eyed and sore-arsed.

Richard hated the harness he had to wear for his bulky hearing aids — he was embarrassed because it looked like a bra.

George Emerson was born in New Brighton, Christchurch, on 6 March 1935. His father, Albert, trained as a schoolteacher and the family moved to Croydon Bush, in rolling farm country northwest of Gore, where Albert ran a one-room school.

The eldest of three children, George had seven years on his brother Les, with another two years back to Alistair. Ingrid describes her in-laws as not being well off.

The defining characters in George Emerson's life were his father and his paternal grandparents, Albert and Ida.

George and his brothers grew up believing the family legend that their grandmother, Ida, was French. Her maiden name was Gay Tan, which if pronounced with a Gallic twist could sound similar to the famous brand of French cigarettes, Gitanes.

The French connection story hid a far more interesting heritage, which the family tried to keep secret. Richard's uncle, Alastair, believed the secrecy helped cover up an inter-racial marriage — frowned on by both Chinese and Pākehā communities at the time — and so Albert could prevent his sons from suffering the same racist bullying he'd been subjected to as a boy.

According to Alistair Emerson, his father could have been mistaken for Asian when he was a young man. 'And it was hinted at by some family members that George, Les and I had done well to "overcome our difficulties".'

Far from French, Ida took half her DNA from her Chinese father, Louis Gay Tan — a pidgin English adaptation of his given name, Looi Yi Tsaan. Born in Canton, he immigrated to New Zealand in 1867, but unlike many Chinese of that period in Otago, he didn't work in the goldfields. Instead Louis established himself as a manager of mine-workers, securing and directing labour where it was needed.

If gold-mining had the ability to make or break fortunes, managing workers became the path to security and steady wealth accumulation, and it saw Louis Gay Tan become one of the better-off and more well-known Chinese in Otago. Just three years after arriving, he became the first Chinese person in the province to become a naturalised New Zealander.

Gay Tan's wealth and position in society allowed him to rise above the typical fate of Chinese gold-miners, many of whom remained poor. He built his own cottage in the mining town of Macraes Flat, about 50 kilometres northwest of Dunedin.

The cottage is still standing and is now listed as a historic place by Heritage New Zealand, which says of it: 'A house of this size, style and permanence was uncommon among European miners, let alone the Chinese. Gay Tan was a man well outside the Chinese norm in Otago, being both relatively wealthy and having married a European wife.'

That European wife was Emma Finch, an English immigrant. Both she and Louis stepped outside racial boundaries to marry at Naseby in 1873. They moved to Macraes Flat in 1875 and had three children, two of whom survived into adulthood. Their daughter Ida — George's grandmother — had a good education and found work as a governess in the household of Dunedin grandee, former New Zealand premier and chief justice, Sir Robert Stout.

The Chinese family connection is a very interesting one and certainly sets us apart from other people. It was natural for me to make fun of this, saying my Chinese comes out when I laugh — you have to see this to understand!

Dad was proud of his Chinese background and wanted to find out more, which led him to Dunedin's authority on Chinese immigrants, James Ng, who assisted him with tracing information.

When George tried to find out about this side of his heritage from his family, he found they wanted nothing to do with their Chinese history, refused to talk about it. Naturally, George was sad about this. Many years ago, it would have been understandable, but in this modern world, multi-racial life is commonplace.

The Gay Tan cottage is only 20 minutes away from my Middlemarch home, I always slow down to view the cottage if I'm on the Macraes Road heading north. Oceania Gold [the local mining company] have made good progress in preserving the cottage. Needless to say, I'm proud that a piece of our early past has been preserved.

Reading the old newspapers revealed that my relatives were hauled in front of court quite a few times for being drunk and disorderly . . . perhaps it was my Chinese blood that led me to setting up a brewery!

George's grandfather Albert fought with the Otago Mounted Rifles in the Boer War then stayed in South Africa to join the Transvaal police. Described by George as an 'explorer', Ida travelled from New Zealand to Great Britain and then to South Africa — where she met and married Albert and the couple had their two sons, Albert Jnr and Horace.

During the First World War, Albert rejoined his old regiment and, with the rank of regimental sergeant major, was deployed to northern France. Ida, meanwhile, left South Africa for New Zealand.

The handwritten Emerson family tree says Ida, on returning with her two sons to New Zealand while Albert fought in the war, was 'not accepted by her father-in-law' because of her Chinese heritage. It gave her son Albert another reason to keep his lineage a secret.

After the war, Albert returned home where he and Ida settled in Canterbury — first in Timaru and then in Christchurch. While Albert's military background instilled in him a fondness for discipline and duty, it was Ida's devout Christianity that saw her share these values with an added dose of devotion. Over the years, she ensured that these three Ds were all instilled into her sons and her grandchildren.

As a result, George's father ran his school with the same military strictness and moral conservatism he learned from his parents. While other pupils could leave it behind at the end of the day, for George there was no escape. He spent morning, noon and night bound to his parents' regime.

Through his early schooling, he found himself in the unenviable position of being a student in his father's classes, which meant higher expectations of his behaviour than of the other children's. He described it once as a 'not terribly comfortable' position. His brother Alistair said their father's discipline was not unjust, but he strapped all his sons on a regular basis at school to ensure no one could accuse him of favouring them.

'I think those strong feelings of discipline carried on into my life, and I think if you speak to my children they will confirm that I've been fairly strong on discipline — perhaps over-strong at times,' George once said. He noted that his father mellowed later in life — as George himself did — but when Richard and Helen were children, he ruled with an iron fist, or rather with a piece of wood in his hand.

'It wasn't brutal,' Helen recalled, 'but I do remember wooden spoons getting broken on Richard's arse. I was scared of Dad. My cousin Catherine, the closest I have to a sister, and I freely admitted to each other we were scared of him. Dad was probably a bit of a bully, but he also had a wicked sense of humour and a fun side to him. For all his gruff exterior, he was incredibly loving and there was no doubt we were in a loving household.'

Even as a practical joker, George preferred scary to funny. A typical example came one evening as the family watched a storm unfold across

Dunedin, lightning flashing in the sky and loud bursts of thunder rocking the house.

Amid the thunderclaps, George exited the room. Shortly afterwards, a monstrous figure with a ghoulish paper bag on his head and dark holes cut out for eyes shuffled into the darkened room. George delighted in the resulting screams of fright.

Another favourite game of George's was Hobgoblins. While out walking in the bush, such as the Pineapple Track up to Flagstaff lookout, George and Richard would race ahead of Ingrid, Helen and any other unwitting family members along for the walk. They would then make use of the track's numerous hiding spots before jumping out on their unsuspecting victims.

Dad was a practical joker, especially when he was at work. One of his favourite tricks was to take a piece of rubber tubing, tie a knot in one end, then drop in a piece of dry ice before tying another knot at the end. He would then walk up to an unwary student and slip the tube into their lab-coat pocket then watch as the student's body heat warmed up the dry ice, causing the tube to swell with carbon dioxide.

I enjoyed these kinds of practical jokes and Dad would often help me create them. Once, I wanted to give my friend Paul Trotman a record voucher for his birthday, but not to make the present too easy to figure out. I explained to Dad that I'd like to use a room in the biochemistry department that was kept at minus 40 degrees to freeze my little project.

With a twinkle in his eyes, George said he liked the idea. The record voucher was triple-sealed in plastic, taped to a broom handle and immersed in a bucket of water inside the freezing-cold room. Boy, what a beautiful 'ice block' it was, with the voucher clearly visible in the middle. Dad was really amused and the ice block was a hit at my mate's party — though he did have to wait several hours to get his hands on the voucher!

George felt isolated during his childhood. The family lived in a remote area and George found it hard to make friends — not helped by his father's school-teacher role. He also felt different to the sons and daughters of farmers in the area and once described himself as a 'townie living a country life'.

Eventually, Albert got a job at Wakari School in Dunedin, and George was able to slip out of his father's shadow at last. That said, he found it hard to adjust to city living. The loner in him found socialising difficult and at Otago Boys' High School he hated the emphasis put on team sports,

particularly rugby. He enjoyed the individualism and solitude of cross-country running, but the school didn't have a team. He fought for the right to run and got permission to join a harrier club outside of school.

'George was non-conformist; he didn't like sport,' his brother Alastair said. 'He wasn't prepared to go along with an all-boys' school culture of rugby and cricket. At one stage, I played cricket and he couldn't understand why I'd want to do that.'

Despite their tough relationship, George and his father bonded over trains and photography. Albert enjoyed photographing ships and locomotives, and at an early age George had a model railway and subscribed to *Meccano Magazine*. 'There were model trains all over the floor of the house,' Alistair said. 'Trains were always an obsession for Dad and George.'

As a boy, George rode his Raleigh Sports bicycle to spots around Dunedin where he could photograph trains. In his final year of high school, he took a bike trip around Southland looking for small branch lines that

George Emerson always carried a camera — or two.

were under threat of closure. His interest in railway infrastructure made him unusual among railway enthusiasts. He understood that the railway era would eventually pass, and the disappearance of trains would in turn signal the end of the infrastructure, the tracks and the stations. He preferred to document that; to capture a disappearing slice of railway life. As such, the Otago Central Railway would become his lifelong passion — for its topography, its sense of history and its place in the community.

On leaving school, George's passion for railway systems spurred him on to apply for a New Zealand Railways scholarship to study engineering. Unsuccessful, he enrolled at Otago University to study chemistry. There he met Ingrid Holst, who also had a railway story running through her DNA — albeit a tragic one.

Her grandfather Olaf Holst came to New Zealand from Denmark after being caught up in a railway accident. In June 1897, Olaf, his parents and three of his six siblings were about to board a train at Gentofte Station, north of Copenhagen, after a family outing. At that moment, an express train missed a stop light and ploughed into the stationary train. In all, 40 people were killed including both of his parents and one of his siblings.

According to Ingrid, Olaf, who was 18 at the time and the eldest child, decided that rather than move in with an aunt and uncle who took custody of the other children, he wanted to 'go as far away from Denmark as possible'. That turned out to be Dunedin.

Somewhat ironically, Olaf's son Erik became a railway engineer and with his wife Catherine had three children: Ingrid, Peter and Richard.

Ingrid Holst grew into a feisty young woman who campaigned for chemistry to be taught at Otago Girls' High School. The school deemed it an unfit subject for young women, but under duress brought in a chemistry teacher for the small group who demanded it. Unfortunately, the school had a teacher but no laboratory, so when Ingrid arrived at Otago University to study chemistry, her knowledge was solely gleaned from books. In modern parlance, she had the software but no proficiency with the hardware.

When Ingrid ended up in a laboratory setting she knew the theory, but the equipment remained foreign to her. Her first task in the lab was an inventory of equipment. 'I asked the boy next to me to explain what was what and he grumbled, "If you've got this far you ought to know that by now." I thought he was the rudest man I'd ever met.'

Rude or not, a spark flew in that chemistry lab and the pair became an item. Ingrid eventually switched to the budding field of biochemistry while George stayed on the chemistry track, getting his Master's degree before switching to biochemistry for his PhD.

Ingrid and George married in 1958 while still at university, and Ingrid later picked up paid work in the biochemistry department. George made a seamless transition from student to lecturer in biochemistry, learning as he went and passing on that knowledge to his students.

Biochemistry delivered an income for George, but his passion — his calling — remained out on the railway lines. In the 1960s he joined the Otago branch of the New Zealand Locomotive and Railway Society (NZLRS), a group set up for railway enthusiasts to get together to exchange stories and photographs.

As part of this group, George gleaned the information required to insert himself into a critical part of New Zealand history. With the country's switch to decimal currency in 1967, a massive, top-secret operation delivered new money to banks around the country. Trains played a critical role in transporting the new currency — the coins in particular weighed far too much to transport by road.

Armed guards accompanied these trains on their secret journeys. Fugitive Great Train Robber Ronnie Biggs was believed (correctly) to be living in Australia, and officials feared that he would come out of hiding to cross the Tasman for a heist.

As a result of the secrecy and the pressure brought to bear on newspaper photographers by police, there was very little documentary evidence of Operation Overland. The *New Zealand Railway Observer* scored a coup over the daily newspapers by publishing an uncredited photo of the 'dollar train' coming into Dunedin.

A half-century later, in 2017, Richard Emerson confirmed the photo had been taken by his father George, who got wind of the train's arrival and snuck out to Ravensbourne to photograph it. There he was briefly apprehended by a police officer and ordered to remove the film from his camera. According to Richard, George always carried two cameras and if any film came out of a camera it was from the 'other' camera!

Previous spread: One of George Emerson's most famous photographs is the 'dollar train' — one of the top-secret trains that carried the decimal currency supply around the country.

With George as chairman, the Otago branch of the NZLRS bought an old steam engine and built a small track for it, creating Dunedin's popular Ocean Beach Railway. That was the first of a number of railway preservation projects, which culminated in the rescue of the famed Taieri Gorge Railway.

As New Zealand Railways scaled back its operation from the 1970s onwards, George led the Otago branch to buy old carriages that had fallen into a derelict state. They planned to restore the smashed windows, rotten woodwork, missing doors and ripped upholstery so they had enough carriages to make a viable train.

As the restoration progressed, the group formed a new incorporated society — the Otago Excursion Train Trust (OETT) — to take over the carriage rebuild programme and run excursions, starting with a jaunt along the increasingly disused Central Otago line from Dunedin to Cromwell in October 1979.

Train projects consumed much of George's spare time. So much so, his daughter Helen remembers the phone being tied up for hours on end in the evenings as George did his wheeling and dealing for what he thought was 'a worthwhile community project'.

Railway historian Bill Cowan said George 'ran a tight ship' with the OETT. He and fellow committee member Arthur Rockliff were the 'action men'.

'Arthur and George had skills that complemented each other so neatly: Arthur was the practical man who spoke and thought NZR lingo and procedure; George had the vision and leadership qualities.'

Over the next few years, the society purchased additional carriages to refurbish and in the summer of 1986–7 around 11,000 passengers were taken to destinations such as Oamaru, Clyde, Kurow, Invercargill and Bluff. On these trips, apart from NZR operating crews, OETT volunteers did everything from handling luggage to cleaning to running the busy buffet car.

The trust recognised the demand for a tourist train from Dunedin through the Taieri Gorge to Middlemarch, and with support from the Dunedin City Council, the first run of the Taieri Gorge Limited chugged off from Dunedin Railway Station on 21 February 1987.

The council later presented George with a framed certificate for his efforts in making the now world-famous train journey a reality — a certificate that later played a role in the creation of one of Emerson's most-loved beers.

FINDING A PLACE IN THE WORLD

The hearing aids I had helped me to hear sounds and to be aware of what was around me, but they didn't help me to understand words. I hated the first set because it looked like I had a bra — those old hearing aids were the size of a cigarette pack and they had to sit in the 'bra', which was a harness my mother made to hold them and which fitted across my chest. It made me feel very self-conscious.

I hated them because they were visible and made me look different to other people. I wanted to be like other people. They were bulky and the sound ran through a wire to an earpiece — it looked like I had a Walkman before anyone had heard of a Walkman.

It was only when I was 11 or 12 that I got the first behind-the-ear hearing aids and the freedom of not wearing that harness was amazing. I was finally able to burn the bra!

While Ingrid built the base for Richard's lip-reading skills with her tireless and focused lessons, others played a vital role in helping her profoundly deaf child not only to communicate but to understand.

Richard had weekly sessions with a speech therapist, Chris Justin, at George Street Normal School. With her, he worked on his pronunciation and the subtleties of inflection and emphasis. She would also pick out words Richard hadn't encountered before and ask him to pronounce them straight off the bat. On problematic words, Chris placed Richard's hand to her throat while she spoke the word, so Richard could feel the vibration in the vocal cords and try to replicate the feeling in his own larynx. Richard struggled with the sensitivity of touch to pick up the small variations in the vocal cord vibration.

Ingrid always made sure Richard was looking directly at her when she was speaking so he could read her lips.

Later, Chris moved to an office on Hanover Street and with that came a technological step that allowed Richard to make a quantum leap. There she had an oscilloscope, described by Richard as having a screen about the size of a large smartphone and resembling a radar. When Chris spoke a word, a pattern reflecting the sound waves came up on the screen and Richard tried to replicate the pattern.

'It was such a vast improvement over the "hands on the throat" technique. I really took that technology on board and I felt this was a huge step forward for me in improving my speech. I still had my days — if I got too tired — when my speech would deteriorate, but I became more aware of and conscious of how I spoke. This was important for me to interact with the normal spoken world.'

John Caselberg also became an invaluable mentor. Having moved from Nelson to Dunedin to study medicine, he became ensconced in the literary and artistic world. Through the fifties and sixties, he became an established poet. His wife Anna was the daughter of renowned painter Toss Woollaston and had once lived with Colin McCahon's family.

For all his artistic merits, it was as a teacher of the deaf that Richard knew John. He became a significant influence in terms of explaining the colloquial meaning of words and phrases. For example, while Richard had learned the word 'excuse' as a reason for not having done his homework, Caselberg might bump into him and say: 'Excuse me!' thereby showing him the word's different contextual uses.

He also taught Richard the rhythm of language, explaining to him that where the emphasis fell in a sentence could determine the meaning of the words in a social context as opposed to their literal meaning. This set Richard on a path towards becoming more eloquent with the English language and helped develop his lifelong love of innuendo and puns. It taught him ways to be witty and play with words, things most people take for granted because they can pick up the most subtle changes in tone or inflection.

But no matter how many words Richard learned to pronounce or puns he could create, the sounds bore little resemblance to what other children knew as normal. Consonants lacked precision, vowel sounds came out squashed, and the overall effect was a flat atonality that made it difficult for others to understand Richard until they got used to listening carefully. On top of that, he struggled with pronunciation, having to take something he'd seen via lips or oscilloscope and turn it into a sound he had never heard.

I think learning about how the vowels are formed with lip movements is an important step into understanding how to lip-read, however the phonic sounds were a real challenge since without hearing it is very difficult to interpret the difference between 'sh' and 'ch'. In fact, it's close to impossible to lip-read the difference.

Over time I've learned to identify the difference in the context of the sentence. But it didn't help me when my primary school mates and I had enjoyed watching *Chitty Chitty Bang Bang* at a special movie premiere for primary schools in Dunedin.

Knowing my speech deficiency, my mates would poke me to recall the name of the movie. I replied innocently, 'Shitty Shitty Bang Bang', and they'd be all laughing. I didn't think the movie was *that* funny, but I agreed with them that it was a bit humorous. Dick Van Dyke was an awesome actor — for me, his character in the movie was one that I could easily lip-read and his animated action helped me even further to understand the story.

When I got home, I told Mum, 'I saw this movie "Shitty Shitty Bang Bang" and my friends thought it was funny.'

I guess my mother understood what they really found so amusing and took pains to explain to me that I wasn't pronouncing it correctly. It then dawned on me that my mates were taking advantage of me!

Mum started working on me to try get the right mouth formation to produce the 'ch' sound. It took me some time to get the hang of it.

Another time, I was travelling with the family on the Northerner express in the North Island in the early 1970s. When the train stopped at Taihape, I tried to pronounce the station name and it would come out wrong. The Māori language took me a while to grasp. Dad pointed to his tie and then to his smiley face — tie-happy — it wasn't perfect but it was close enough!

Naturally there was a lot of frustration in trying to understand other kids my age. Not surprisingly my frustration led to some fights. Some of the taunts could be quite demeaning. Rob Smillie had just arrived into Maori Hill primary school, and it wasn't long before he picked out that I was a little different from the rest of the children in the classroom.

When the class broke for recess, Rob would seek me out and start to taunt me by saying, 'Deafy, deafy'. It made my blood boil, but he wouldn't stop.

My frustration got so bad that I lashed out and punched him in the eye!

Hoo boy, Rob got a real shiner and, of course, a few words from his father about treating a deaf kid that way.

Funnily enough, we became best friends — what a way to start a friendship! I got into lots of fights back then — I had a bad temper and people kept winding me up. I didn't like being taunted. Fighting was my way of showing them that I wasn't a weakling. I wanted to prove myself. It would be silly of me to shy away when people were being cruel to me.

Rob Smillie will never forget the day Richard Emerson punched him in the face — and he knew he deserved it.

Rob's father Alistair was a professor of oral pathology, and the family arrived in Dunedin when Rob was eight. That was when he started at Maori Hill School and encountered a deaf boy who spoke strangely. 'I remember seeing him in the playground, and he looked quite different to anyone else with these things sticking out of his ears. Because he was deaf and couldn't talk very well people thought he wasn't that smart — but as I was to learn he was very imaginative and creative.

'I was teasing him when I first met him, calling him terrible names like "deafy" and generally giving him a hard time. He promptly smacked me in the face and gave me a black eye. I thought, "Hang on, here's a kid with some moxie. Here's a guy who's prepared to stand up for himself!" I'd thought he was a quiet boy, but he had a real spirit there. I decided he was a pretty interesting bloke, and that was the start of 40-plus years of friendship.'

Other friends didn't bat an eyelid when Richard biffed Rob; those who had been around him long enough knew he had a short fuse, one born of frustration on various levels. His hearing aids made Richard feel self-conscious or ashamed and, from time to time, they created a feedback screech or whistle that irritated both Richard and those around him. Mostly, he reacted to other children's cruel teasing. 'He did get teased,' said Grant Hanan, who started at Maori Hill School at the same time as Richard and would go on to become a lifelong friend.

'Every so often things exploded and you knew about it — he would often fly off the handle. And Richard was always quite physical. He loved bullrush for the physical contact — he was fully up for all that.'

Richard and Grant both went to Boys' Brigade, which Hanan remembered as being run by 'a strict ex-army guy' who doubled as the local butcher. He ran a military-style outfit with a lot of drill. 'With Richard, there was an element of trying to tame the beast a little bit.'

After their initial fight, Richard and Rob became inseparable friends, their lives defined by adventure, comic books, music and trouble-making. Rob also became Richard's 'translator'.

'We always had to face each other to talk — he was a good lip-reader, but you had to enunciate quite clearly,' says Rob. 'A lot of people found it hard to understand Richard because of his atonality, so I would play the role of translator or broker with others. We never treated Richard differently and in some ways were a little harder on him.

———

HE COULD CONNECT BETTER WITH ADULTS BECAUSE AT LEAST ADULTS KNEW TO LOOK AT HIM WHEN THEY WERE SPEAKING. OTHER CHILDREN DIDN'T ALWAYS UNDERSTAND THAT HE COULDN'T BE PART OF THEIR CONVERSATION IF THEY WEREN'T LOOKING AT HIM.

———

'You could see and share his frustration at what being deaf was like. You could understand his handicap, and then accept it, break through it and eventually take advantage of it. In the end, I didn't even think of him as deaf.'

When he was eight, Mike Hormann's family shifted into Dunedin from Mosgiel and he joined Richard's class at Maori Hill School. 'We got on quite well at school. Between Richard and George, they had quite a few train sets and that was great for other young boys. We always had some fun at Richard's expense but I can't recall anyone being nasty because he wasn't that kind of guy. He got a little bit of special attention — but not in a bad way.'

Another friend reckoned Richard didn't mind the teasing because it brought attention — something he struggled to get from most children. Other kids either didn't understand they had to look at Richard when they spoke or they couldn't be bothered making the effort. As a result, he felt excluded from a lot of conversations and groups.

According to his mother, 'He was a lonesome boy in many ways. He could connect better with adults because at least adults knew to look at him when they were speaking. Other children didn't always understand that he couldn't be part of their conversation if they weren't looking at him. That's why he's developed a habit of trying to control the conversation, so he knows what people are talking about.'

Even when people did remember to look at Richard, it didn't guarantee they'd be understood.

I still struggle with lip-reading, especially meeting new people for the first time and trying to get a feel of the person's way of talking, trying to recognise how people form familiar words in their own way, trying to get a hang of their 'accent'. Some people are naturally easy to read, others can fall into the moderate and bloody hard categories.

With the 'moderate' people, once I have been reading them for some time I get the hang of it, but I sometimes have to ask them to repeat things to grasp the meaning of the sentence. With the 'bloody hard' ones I tend to nod, agreeing with whatever they are mumbling about and hoping I haven't been asked a direct question. For that reason, I tend to steer well away from 'bloody hard' ones as these people, through no fault of their own, are too hard to understand. They make me feel uncomfortable, I lose my confidence and I want to walk away or talk to an 'easy' person.

To avoid upsetting people who have come a long way to visit the brewery, another method I use is to ask a workmate with an 'easy face' to be with me. When I stumble trying to understand a newcomer, the workmate will sense that I am struggling and will repeat what the person is trying to tell me. It's like having an interpreter.

I've also learnt that I can politely say: 'Excuse me, I am deaf. Could you please look at me so I can read your lips?' They will then quite naturally change the way they talk and often I will find this much easier.

Richard and Rob devoured the English comics of the day — such as *Whizzer and Chips*, and *Beano* — and became devotees of *The Adventures of Tintin*. They thought Richard's father George looked and behaved like the *Tintin* character Captain Haddock, with his bushy beard and fierce temper. As a result, the boys ran around shouting 'bashi-bazouk' and 'billions of bilious blue blistering barnacles!' George in turn shouted at them to 'stop acting the giddy goat!' — a phrase he used so often it's burned into Smillie's memory.

These comic books inspired Richard and Rob to create their own strip, *The Snoots and The Grunts*, about a space-travelling set of families. Richard, who had an eye for detail and an artist's touch, drew the pictures while Rob wrote the dialogue.

The mischievous inspiration of *Dennis the Menace* meant poor Ingrid bore the brunt of their practical jokes, like the time they rigged a bucket of water over the half-open basement door and told her the cat had gone down there to be sick. Ingrid ran downstairs only to get drenched as the bucket tipped on her head.

Ingrid laughed off the pranks, but not so George. As a result, the boys' rebellious streak would vaporise when he appeared.

'We were petrified of George,' Rob recalled. 'George was a strict disciplinarian and, to be honest, everyone was scared of him. I think he saw me as a bad influence on Richard. I think today I'd have been diagnosed with ADHD, but back then we were being sent out of the classroom a lot. Notes were going back to parents and George was concerned about our relationship.'

Rob and his other mates did their best to have fun with Richard's ability to lip-read and would also take advantage of his mercurial swiftness to anger. Rob, for instance, would noiselessly mouth things like 'You're an idiot' across the room to Richard. He would respond with a shake of his fist or some choice words of his own, often spoken too loudly. He would then be admonished by the teacher: 'Richard, what is going on? Calm down!'

At primary school, the pair often ended up down in the hall to be disciplined. Later, when they left Maori Hill to attend Balmacewen Intermediate School, their disruptiveness saw them sent to different classrooms for their own good.

Richard was not always the innocent, easily agitated victim. He was sometimes also the architect of his own fate. On one occasion, he drew a picture of their teacher sitting on a toilet. The small sketch went from hand to hand around the classroom until the teacher caught one of them red-handed. 'She was not amused and I got sent out for a moment with the headmaster,' Richard said.

It may have been on that trip down the corridor to visit the headmaster that Richard showed his anti-authoritarian side. When asked by his friends what had happened, Richard shrugged. He'd turned off his hearing aids and lowered his gaze — he hadn't heard or seen a word of the reprimand dished out to him!

Professional wrestling fascinated the boys — Richard loved its physicality and enjoyed demonstrating his considerable strength. One day, Rob got a little too boisterous and slammed Richard to the ground, knocking him unconscious. When he came to, he looked at Rob and asked why he'd come around to the Emerson house. He had no idea what had happened. When Ingrid came home, Rob had to explain the situation because Richard still remembered nothing.

After a quick trip to the hospital, Richard got a cautionary all-clear, but Ingrid had to wake him every hour during the night to make sure he hadn't suffered a concussion.

In the morning, a tired but none-the-wiser Richard woke up to his mother's inquiry: 'How are you feeling?'

'Fine,' came his reply.

His sister Helen then popped her head in and asked, 'How are you?'

'Fine!'

Down at breakfast, George asked, 'Are you feeling all right?'

'I'm fine!!!'

At school that morning, Rob's first words to Richard were, 'How are you feeling?'

'Everyone's asking me that and I don't know why!'

While Richard loved physicality, sport didn't work for him. He did, however, find a passion for riding his bike as fast as possible.

I didn't play much sport. I tried rugby, but it was a little bit problematic as to play it I had to take my hearing aids out. The first time I played, I grabbed the ball and ran across the field, thinking, 'This is great, no one can tackle me!' But I didn't realise the whistle had been blown. So, rugby wasn't a very good idea for me.

When we were kids, we all had push bikes and I loved to ride my bike fast. One day, my friends suggested we have a race around the grounds at John McGlashan College, a private school near where we lived. We were all on our bikes at the start line and someone said 'Ready, set, go!'

I raced off, pedalling as hard as I could. I was ahead, I was in front. I couldn't hear anything because the wind in my hearing aids was so loud. I knew I was pedalling hard because my back wheel was spinning in the wet grass; I was going to win this race.

I looked behind me and . . . faark! . . . There was no one there. My mates were nowhere to be seen. Suddenly, someone reached out and grabbed at my shoulder. It was the school's groundskeeper. He asked me what I thought I was doing.

'I was having a bike race . . .' and I looked around for the others only to find I was by myself.

'Get off that bike and walk!' was his response. He then followed me out of the school grounds and up the road a bit.

I kept on walking until I came across my friends sitting outside the dairy laughing their heads off. It was then I realised what had happened. They knew I'd get caught by the groundskeeper, the bastards!

While it was another example of me being naïve and gullible and then ashamed, the irony is that having people play tricks on me like that helped me socially. I was always inquisitive and liked being with people who were fun, but when I was younger those same people would get me into trouble because I was a bit naïve. I became a source of amusement for them. If I had gone to a school for the deaf, I don't think I would have developed the same social skills that I did.

Teasing and misbehaviour aside, Richard's schooling remained normal, but his home life had some marked differences to those of his peers.

For starters, the Emerson family didn't have a television — much to Helen's ongoing annoyance. George had no time for TV, regarding it as frivolous.

Actually, the family did briefly have a television, which was given to them by Ingrid's parents. Richard enjoyed watching the newsreader Philip Sherry, but little else.

'He could lip-read Philip Sherry word for word because his face filled most of the screen,' Ingrid recalled. 'The reason my parents got us a TV was for Richard to watch cartoons and other children's programmes, but he never seemed interested. I said to him, "Don't you like that?" He replied, "No, they just go baa, baa, baa." Of course, we then realised that you can't lip-read cartoons, so he didn't enjoy them.'

Much to George's satisfaction, the television then disappeared.

Helen, of course, saw things differently. 'The one thing that was different in our family is that we never had a TV when I was growing up.

Previous spread: Richard and Helen in the Netherlands in 1974. George went on a sabbatical to Leicester and the family took the opportunity to travel through Europe.

That was in part because Richard couldn't follow what was going on; and later when it was suggested to my father that I might enjoy TV, he said it was all rubbish anyway. "We're not having television in my house," he'd say.

'It was quite traumatic for me — everyone else at school would be talking about what was on TV last night and I couldn't join in that conversation. I would read the *Listener* to get synopses of stories just to join in the conversation. I didn't blame Richard for it — and I never felt sorry for him — it was just the way it was: we didn't have a TV because Richard couldn't understand it.'

The next television that came into the house was bought by Richard himself after he'd left school and started working.

'Teletext must have just come in in the mid-eighties and there were some shows with closed captions,' Helen said. 'I think we were the only family that watched *'Allo 'Allo!* with the subtitles done to reflect the fake French accents — that's something most people don't know, because who would watch *'Allo 'Allo!* with subtitles?! But it opened up a whole new world for Richard.'

The lessons from John Caselberg, the teasing from his friends and even what he learned from watching TV made Richard hyper-aware of body language and what it can add to a conversation. For a lip-reader, 'listening' to someone with an expressive face can change the dynamic — a twinkle in the eye will indicate a joke, a glower will emphasise a verbal telling-off. One of the hardest things for Richard was trying to understand people with deadpan faces. He much preferred his friends and his TV characters to be exuberant and animated.

I used to go to the movies, but I could never pick up the dialogue. Anything with lots of dialogue is very hard to follow — but action movies are okay. When videos came out I would hunt around the video shop looking for movies with subtitles that I could watch, but that wasn't always easy.

When DVDs came out — oh my god! — most of them came with subtitles and that was it for me. I loved it. Even better, Netflix. Life gets better as technology moves along. I've been able to go back and watch early movies and pick up the innuendo and inside jokes. I love the British comedies and my favourite is probably *Death at a Funeral*.

Long before subtitles, there was one show I could watch easily and I would watch a lot — *Some Mothers Do 'Ave 'Em* with Michael Crawford as Frank Spencer.

He was very visual. He had an expressive face and moved a lot, going 'Oooohh, ooohhh!' It was quite dramatic.

I rely on body language a lot — I cannot pick up sarcasm in the way people speak, but I can pick it up from their body language and expressions. I'm not very good with people who do things with a straight face. I tend to stay away from deadpan faces as I can't tell if they are pissed off with me or unhappy about something. It's like trying to lip-read the radio. You can't tell what mood somebody is in if the face is deadpan.

I can tell when people feel uncomfortable before they speak by the way they are moving or holding themselves. It's not something that can be taught. People who have natural facial expressions are great for me. Rob Smillie was one of those people — he had a face I could easily read and that helped me a lot. I'm more inclined to be with people who are expressive and outgoing. I probably spend more time with extroverted people and not with people who have a radio face.

In 1974, George took a year's sabbatical and the family moved to Leicester in England. The trip threatened to undo much of 10-year-old Richard's learning as he was dropped into a foreign environment and a school system not attuned to his deafness.

Richard and Helen in Cologne, Germany.

He had inordinate trouble with a teacher from Ireland. Trying to lip-read a new 'accent' presented enough difficulty on its own, but the teacher was also an incessant cigarette smoker. As such, he'd developed a way of talking out of the side of his mouth that allowed him to smoke and talk at the same time. He also had a fiery temper. He and Richard failed to understand each other, resulting in heated clashes during Richard's short time at the school and little successful learning.

Through it all, Richard learned a valuable lesson in the subtle variations of the English language. After time he could adjust to the Midlands accent and by the time he returned to New Zealand his own 'English' accent had changed as a result of trying to make himself understood.

Ingrid tells the story of Richard coming home from school at Leicester and she asked him what he'd had for lunch. 'Harm and airgs,' came his reply.

WHEN DVDS CAME OUT — OH MY GOD! — MOST OF THEM CAME WITH SUBTITLES AND THAT WAS IT FOR ME. I LOVED IT. EVEN BETTER, NETFLIX. LIFE GETS BETTER AS TECHNOLOGY MOVES ALONG.

I've learnt over the years how the vowels can change with accents and how foreign people show the vowels differently. I could lip-read Americans as they had this long drawl on the 'a' vowels and a tendency to stretch the words out somewhat, making the word I know seem much longer than it is.

When we were living in Leicester in 1974, I had to attend Lindon Junior Primary School. Initially, it was strange being in this school where everyone spoke quite differently. The words were there, but they sounded odd. It took me a wee while to grasp the local dialect. Words like the model train manufacturer 'Hornby' sounded like 'Hon-bee' and 'cup of tea' came out like 'coup o teeea'.

Back in New Zealand after a year in the UK, my mother noticed that I had taken on a slight English accent. Recently, I impressed my workmates when I was listening to/lip-reading an English woman at the brewery. After a few moments, I asked her if she was from Yorkshire. Taken aback, she said, 'Why, yes, I am. How did you know?'

I explained that I had lived in the UK for some time and had got to know some of the dialects that could be lip-read. My workmates were gobsmacked and disbelieving, wondering 'How can Richard pick this up?'

While the gift of a television from his grandparents didn't quite work out for Richard, another present they gave him hit the spot. They bought Richard a large tape deck — with the idea he'd play music on it — but instead he used it to record the sound of steam engines onto blank cassettes.

'He loved the rhythm of the engine,' Helen said, 'and he'd record these trains for his listening pleasure at home afterwards — the problem was he played it so loud the rest of us had to listen to it as well.'

Ingrid's parents also gave Richard his first taste — and love — of beer. Erik and Catherine Holst bought an old railway house in Bainesse, a location too small to even call itself a village, between Palmerston North and Himatangi Beach. The house, which sat on a large section, had been abandoned after a highway had been rerouted. It became the Holst holiday house during Ingrid's childhood and later her parents retired there.

When Richard was 10, he got his first taste of beer, a sip of his grandfather's home brew, when visiting Bainesse one summer. 'We were cutting grass with a scythe,' he remembers. 'And Grandfather came down the path carrying a tray of glasses and a bottle of beer. I can still remember that first taste of beer — bitter but malty.'

It's no surprise Richard remembered the moment so well — even at a young age he had an obsession with food and flavours. When he was young, an Indian family lived next door to the Emersons. The Mukherjee family had come to Otago from Sweden. Their daughter Sutapa was a year younger than Richard to the day. Richard loved the smells that would waft from next door and he developed a taste for Indian food from an early age. The more spicy and garlicky the better.

Another family introduced the Emersons to Thai green curry, which Richard kept demanding his mother make. Macadamia nuts introduced by another biochemistry staffer who arrived from Hawaii tantalised Richard's taste buds. He also loved walking around Dunedin smelling the odours

of the city —the Cadbury chocolate factory, the instant coffee production at Gregg's, where he would later work, and the produce at the Chinese greengrocers.

He also had access to one of this country's culinary giants — his aunt, Alison Holst. As Alison Payne, she'd grown up in Dunedin, the eldest of three now-famous sisters: Clare Ferguson is a London-based food stylist and writer, and Patricia Payne is a renowned opera singer. While studying home science at Otago, Alison met Ingrid's brother Peter, who was studying medicine, and the pair married. She was then plucked from nowhere to do cooking demonstrations on television, replacing the original Kiwi celebrity chef, the Galloping Gourmet, Graham Kerr. Alison and Peter were among the first shareholders in the brewery.

A lot of people don't know Alison Holst is my aunty. I remember going up to her place in Karori in Wellington. She had a small kitchen at the back of the house, but she didn't stay in the kitchen. She'd bring the chopping board into the lounge and chop vegetables while talking to us. She was always well-spoken — she was an impressive woman, very dynamic.

An extended family portrait, including New Zealand's first celebrity chef, Alison Holst (third from right at the back), who married Ingrid's brother Peter Holst (holding the baby).

Richard and Helen.

I loved the way she was able to make food from what you had in the cupboard rather than having to get exotic ingredients — she came up with recipes that actually worked. Her son, Simon, my cousin, is very good too, especially his bread recipes.

I was aware at a young age that I had a better sense of smell than other people. I loved spices and garlic. To me, smell and taste was a language. It tells a story and can be quite exciting. I love the smell of coal from the steam engines.

Smell in food helped me to think of flavours in beer. Once, I had a bottle of gueuze — a Belgian-style sour beer, pronounced gooze — and it had a smell that I knew was a smell from my childhood in Dunedin. I had this memory of a smell, but I couldn't for the life of me remember where it was from. It wasn't from another beer — I knew it was from my childhood. I was thinking, 'Where have I smelt that?' but I couldn't get it.

Then a couple of weeks later — Eureka! Eureka! It was from the Kingston Flyer. There's a balcony carriage called the birdcage with five or six small compartments each with leather seats. When you sat down a puff of air came out — Whap! — and this smell came with it. The seats were stuffed with horse hair and that was the smell of the gueuze. That's how evocative a sense of smell can be — until then, I'd never thought of connecting a bottle of beer with the Kingston Flyer!

Richard embraced trains wholeheartedly — the size, noise, smell, heat, the clouds of steam, the visceral nature of giant gasping, puffing beasts — appealed to the side of his personality that also loved textured, operatic music. For a long time, he dreamed of becoming a steam train driver but soon realised he'd been born in the wrong time for such a calling. By the time he was old enough to operate a train, steam engines had gone, replaced by diesel and electric engines, and to be certified, train drivers needed good hearing because much of the operation relied on radio communication.

Richard made do instead with model railways. His original set, a gift from Santa one Christmas, included a little blue tank engine and a few wagons that looped his bedroom floor. His grandparents also had a small train set that had belonged to George and his brothers. It had two parallel tracks circling each other and it gave Richard hours of amusement as he tried to build a train long enough so the engine could almost 'catch its tail'.

Over a period of years, George dug out a basement under the family home to create a new laundry, an extra toilet and a photographic darkroom. Using a pick and shovel he carted countless wheelbarrow-loads of soil up to a skip.

Once cleared, George saw the space had room for a model railway, which was duly set up. Richard spent hours in that room reading through the vast collection of model railway magazines his father and grandfather had accrued over the years.

The railway construction helped Richard develop the kind of problem-solving skills he'd need when he started his brewery operation on the whiff of some old hops a few years later. It also created an environment where he could work at his own pace, teaching himself at a comfortable but meticulous speed in contrast to what felt like the flurry of instructions he received at school.

As an educational tool, the model railway proved invaluable, with Richard teaching himself basic electrical wiring, soldering and woodwork. He designed the track layout, incorporating a rack railway to take the train up a steep incline, designed as a reminder of a family holiday to the Swiss Alps in 1974. To recreate the setting, Richard built an alpine mountain out of chicken wire, plaster of Paris and foam rubber. When completed, it was so high it almost touched the ceiling.

He covered a frame of wood and chicken wire with papier-mâché. Over that he whipped up batches of plaster of Paris to smear over the papier-mâché. He created vertical rock faces using tinfoil from his mother's kitchen as a mould, filling it with plaster and removing the foil when it was semi-dry. His most challenging task came when he decided to put clumps of green tussock on the side of the mountain. One of his magazines suggested using foam rubber that had been dyed green.

Para Rubber was the first stop to buy the right kind of foam, not the polystyrene bubble stuff, but the stuff they use to make foam mattresses. The next step was to cut the foam into fine pieces. First, I cut it into small chunky bits with scissors then I put them in my mother's blender . . . At first, it was interesting to observe the dry foam bouncing off the sharp blades. Hmmm, I needed to try something else to render the bits smaller. I thought, 'Why not freeze the foam with water then whizz it?'

Yes, that was a step in the right direction, though it took a while for the foam to dry out. The final step was to dye the blitzed foam with green clothes dye . . .

Bingo! I'd done it!

But I couldn't use my mother's blender for much longer as I could see she wasn't impressed with little bits of foam lingering around the kitchen. However, my education was complete: I'd learnt something and got it right!

That model railway was an important part of my growing up. Unfortunately, it fell into disrepair the moment I started developing Emerson's Brewery as the time available for working on it became less and less. There would be the rare occasion where Dad and I would have a beer or two and run a few trains over the layout.

One of the last times we operated the layout together was when George was still able to venture down to the basement. He was suffering from a brain tumour and his balance was not that good. We ran his favourite little acquisition, a scale model New Zealand Railways F Class steam locomotive. It was a pleasure to operate it for him, though a little painful for me to see him struggling to appreciate the little engine because he couldn't see too well at that time.

Richard was always happy when he was around trains.

DUNEDIN SOUNDS

I couldn't grasp information if I couldn't see it. It was extremely difficult and frustrating at high school — that's why I liked to work on the model railway because I could teach myself in my own time. At high school, you had to have everything done in a certain time frame — there were deadlines for work, exams that you had to study towards — that's why I had two years of sixth form, it took me that long to get all the information.

Richard loved the Dunedin music scene – in all its forms.

Richard went to Logan Park High School for two reasons — one, his father George had hated his experience at Otago Boys' High School, and two, George and Ingrid felt that the relatively new, co-ed school would be better for Richard's socialisation and personal development than an all-boys' school that had a strong emphasis on sport.

Like so many steps in Richard's life, the transition from intermediate school to high school took him out of his comfort zone. He went from the relative security of small schools, primary and intermediate, close to home and with familiar teachers and friends who knew him and who he in turn could read well. Suddenly, he found himself at a bigger school and without some of his trusted allies, such as Rob Smillie and Mike Hormann, who had gone to Otago Boys' High School.

With a bunch of new teachers and new classmates, and at the awkward adolescent age, high school became a difficult and isolating experience for Richard. He struggled to keep up with the pace of teaching, with having a different teacher for each subject, each with a unique style and an individual accent he had to master. Lack of familiarity with Richard's needs meant many talked to a blackboard instead of facing him, leaving him to ask classmates for help or copying notes by looking over someone's shoulder. He soon learned to sit beside students who had fast and neat writing.

In the summer between his third- and fourth-form years, tragedy struck the school. According to Ingrid, Richard 'adored' Logan Park's headmaster Arch Wilson. Returning at the start of his fourth-form year to the news Wilson had died over the summer holidays devastated Richard. Wilson had been climbing on Mt Aspiring and had gone missing.

Arch Wilson was the first principal of Logan Park High School. When I first met him, I felt in awe — he inspired confidence and warmth and gave me a great welcome to the school. Mr Wilson was a visionary leader, the right person at the right time for a new high school. He treated us students with respect and made you feel that you were part of a great school team. His loss in the Mt Aspiring climbing incident in 1980 was a hard one to accept and even harder to come to terms with as his body was never found.

Educational difficulties aside, Richard's school years bore a striking resemblance to those of most other Kiwi teenage boys — trying to summon the courage to ask a girl out on a date, discovering beer, buying a first car and listening to music. But when you're deaf, well, none of that comes easy.

For a start, he couldn't hear music the way others did. He couldn't ring up girls and ask them out on a date. Learning to drive, in a manual car as the rules required, presented all sorts of problems — from not hearing the engine's noise to missing things such as fire engine sirens. Beer, however, presented fewer problems.

'Richard was fun,' said long-time friend David Stedman, who enjoys the sense of adventure Richard brings to everything in his life.

'If you were around Richard chances are you would be taken somewhere, you'd learn something or he'd show you something. He drew people to him. He was always exploring, always up to something. He'd lead you up some crazy, scrubby hill — pulling you into places you never thought you'd go, and once you got there you'd be grateful because there would be an amazing vista.

'Other times it felt as if it was hard to break through to him — sometimes it felt like he chose to be like that. But he had an amazing way of being self-effacing — he injected humour into everything. He amazed me.'

Richard and David became good friends when Richard repeated his sixth-form year at Logan Park. 'We grew up in a similar area of Dunedin and I knew Richard because he was a memorable guy — his deafness and that shock of blond hair made you aware of him.'

The pair bonded over music and trains — specifically model railways. Stedman admitted they were nerdy kids who loved the authenticity of the model railways, and Stedman loved the track Richard had built in the family basement.

Stedman, along with his brothers Stephen and Darren, became an integral part of the Dunedin music scene, which also drew in Richard.

I prefer music that has a certain dynamic range, that's interesting, theatrical, operatic . . . it started with Split Enz, Genesis, Pink Floyd, The Beatles and later the Dunedin bands, like The Chills and The Verlaines. I used to go to the Dunedin pubs — the Oriental, the Captain Cook, the Empire. I could feel the music.

'Pink Frost' from The Chills, with its unusual start, was a great song. The Verlaines, their song 'Baud to Tears' — 'They go down, they drown' — I loved that. Graeme Downes's music was like an opera. They'd start quietly and music would build. And Straitjacket Fits — they were awesome and powerful. Shayne Carter was a great singer to follow as he had a powerful voice and used it to great effect.

Richard's photos of The Verlaines in the early 1980s. Richard loves the 'Dunedin Sound' so much he named a beer after The Verlaines album *Bird Dog*, top right, and The Chills, bottom right, have played at two brewery openings.

Some other singers didn't use their vocals so well — they would mumble and I didn't like that.

Of all the things about Richard Emerson, the thing most people struggle to fathom is his love of music.

'Music? As a deaf boy, how does that work? I know he feels the rhythm, feels the music — but it wasn't the same to him as the rest of us,' Stedman said.

Martin Phillipps, frontman for The Chills, went to school with Richard at Logan Park. 'I still don't fully understand his love of music. I want to know: what is he actually hearing? He talks about feeling the bass in his chest — which is something we all feel — but he can distinguish his favourite songs, so it's more complex than that.'

OF ALL THE THINGS ABOUT RICHARD EMERSON, THE THING MOST PEOPLE STRUGGLE TO FATHOM IS HIS LOVE OF MUSIC.

It started in the mid-seventies when Deep Purple's 'Smoke on the Water' — with its trademark opening bassline — captured Richard's attention. He sought out similar big, anthemic bands, skipping over anything light and sugary; music that barely touched the sides didn't interest him, he wanted the full spectrum of sound.

With his good friend Rob Smillie as a guide, he would listen to albums as Rob ran his finger along the lyrics to help Richard better understand the songs. Rob would point out when the instruments changed, when the vocals kicked in.

Noting his appreciation of music, Ingrid enrolled Richard in piano lessons. He spent a year learning piano, but couldn't officially progress any further because the grade one exam featured an ear test, which he had no chance of passing. Yet he loved the lessons for helping 'make use of what I've got — it helped me differentiate sounds. I stopped when I was around fourteen, but it was probably one of the best things I have ever done — it helped me appreciate music a lot more.'

Richard reinforced Ingrid's belief in the lessons when he came home from school one day as his mother was listening to the Concert programme on Radio New Zealand. 'He said: "Music, Mum, and fast." It showed he could pick up the tempo.'

In order to gain maximum enjoyment from his music, Richard needed to listen with the volume turned up to the maximum, creating its own set of problems for the rest of the Emerson household. According to his sister Helen, 'The whole house would vibrate and you were forced to listen to whatever Richard was listening to.'

George disapproved of rock music, seeing it as a shallow pleasure, but nevertheless agreed to fork out for a record player. Richard duly signed the family up to the World Record Club, a mail-order subscription-based business from which LPs could be ordered at low prices.

The one problem Richard has with music is the need to listen to it with no other sounds in the background.

I have to be totally focused and still to absorb it all. If there are other noises the sounds tend to move around — my brain cannot separate the music from the other background sounds. If I'm in the car, I can't play music because the background noise from the road blends in with the music and muffles it. I don't know how normal hearing people can listen to music in the car with all the road noise.

I like the purity of listening to music with nothing else around. Technology has also helped as I can use Bluetooth to turn my hearing aids into earplugs to play music, but I have to turn the volume up and other people complain they get distracted by what I'm listening to.

The burgeoning local music scene, which became known as the Dunedin Sound, gave Richard a chance to combine his love of music with his passion for photography. Despite being underage, this saw him take his camera to bars such as the Oriental, the Empire and the Captain Cook to photograph the bands of the time.

Stedman, whose later career as a bookbinder would help inspire the beer of that name, played in a band called In A Circle in the early 1980s. Richard would hang out at the band practice room, taking photographs and enjoying the urgent, raw nature of the music they played.

At one stage, In A Circle recorded two tracks to be included on a proposed second volume of the famed *Dunedin Double* EP, which launched

The Verlaines, The Chills, The Stones and Sneaky Feelings. Richard took the photographs of the band to run on the album cover, but for various reasons the EP never got produced and Richard's career as an entertainment photographer ended before it began.

It's not too much of a stretch to say Dunedin music — particularly at Logan Park High School — had an indirect influence on Richard's brewing career.

As a modern school, close to the university campus and connected tangentially to the student scene, Logan Park became a hotbed of musical and artistic talent. Many well-known musicians came through the school — including Phillipps and his sister Rachel, both of whom were in The Chills; Graeme Downes, Darren Stedman and Jane Dodd who all played in The Verlaines; The Rip's Alastair Galbraith and Robbie Muir; and Andrew Brough from Straitjacket Fits, The Orange and Bike. Such was Richard's love of Dunedin, he later released a series of beers honouring some of his favourite tracks — 'Tally Ho' by The Clean, 'North by North' by The Bats and 'Bird Dog' by The Verlaines.

Immersed in this post-punk counter-culture, Richard and his friends, such as David Stedman and Phil Hurring, another Dunedin musician, took

George's sabbatical to Scotland in 1983 was life-changing for 18-year-old Richard, as that's where he discovered good beer.

an anti-establishment view on many things — including beer.

They spurned Speight's as the local drop — and any beer from Lion, the country's biggest brewery, was considered the thing budding rebels were most loath to drink. Photos from In A Circle band practices show cans of Leopard Strong Ale, evidence the youngsters preferred to experiment; to feel as if they weren't sheep.

As a symbol of how badly they viewed Lion, Richard gets teased to this day for having made the grave mistake of buying a crate of Lion Brown when sent into a bottle store to score for his mates.

'As teenagers we used to send in Richard to buy the beer — I don't know why we thought he would be successful, maybe his unusual speech made him seem older . . . Whatever the reason, we'd send him off and sit with our fingers crossed and he usually came back with the goods,' David Stedman said.

'But this one day, he was sent in to get DB and he came back with Lion Brown. We were outraged that he could have made such a mistake. Later, when he was in Edinburgh during his dad's sabbatical, I used to see ads in the *Otago Daily Times* for Lion Brown and I would cut them out and post them to Richard — no letter, nothing — just the advertisement. I did that a number of times, much to Richard's ongoing annoyance.

'Even years later, if he was in the middle of conversation and I wanted to trip him up, I would mouth it to him, "Lion Brown". It was a big mistake and he paid.'

From an early age, with my friends I had to be independent. I couldn't ring them up on the phone because I couldn't hear them. I had to walk around to their house and physically see them. I had to knock on the door and ask if they wanted to come out and play. That helped cement my early friendships because I had to see the people. But I'm not naturally outgoing.

The downside of that in my teenage years was that I had no girlfriends because I couldn't ring them up and say, 'Will you go out with me?' and I couldn't ask anyone to ring up a girl for me because I didn't want them to know about my relationships. I was very private about that. Some girls were nice enough to invite me out to their places, but I didn't have much luck in that area.

Richard's inability to use the telephone made life both interesting and complicated in the Emerson household. He took a couple of approaches to the phone — in one, he would dial a friend and ask if he could come around without ever being certain he would understand the answer; the other involved getting Helen to make his calls.

'He used to ring me at home asking if he could come around,' said Stedman, 'and I'd be saying as clearly as possible "Yes" or "No", but it was never a conversation. I'd be going "NO! NO!" but it was fifty-fifty as to whether he would get the message. You were never sure, so you had to brace yourself for him coming around despite the fact you said "No". But it summed up Richard. He was not afraid to try to overcome his disability — he didn't let the idea that he wasn't able to use the phone stop him from using the phone.'

Helen hated her role as personal assistant but felt she had no choice. 'I found it incredibly hard as a young girl to have to call these older boys. I didn't resent it; I just knew Richard needed someone to do it. It was like doing homework; you didn't like it, but you knuckled down and did it. And as a little sister, I thought I was doing something nice for my big brother.'

She'd be embarrassed when someone other than Richard's friend answered the phone and she'd hear them saying: 'Ooooh, it's a girl for you,' and Helen would shout: 'No, no, it's Richard's sister, it's actually Richard calling.'

She would then have a conversation, relaying messages back and forth by mouthing the words to Richard who would lip-read her silent responses. The brother and sister got so good at this type of communication they could 'talk' to each other across a crowded room.

. . .

Where Richard was stymied in his pursuit of teenage love, he was gung-ho in all other aspects of his life — he was always on the go, exploring, bashing through the bush with his mates, rushing to look around the next corner.

He thrived on the physical contact of bullrush and wrestling, but the competitor in Richard needed an outlet, which he found on his Healing 10-speed bike. As a teenager, he had various methods of getting to school, including a 30-minute walk, but he preferred biking, swooping down from his home high in the hills towards Logan Park High School on the flat.

There was a little bit of resistance from my father about the gooseneck handlebars I'd originally chosen for my bike, so I had to compromise by installing the normal bike bars, but once that was done I discovered speed.

Hoo boy! I could get to school so quick as the chosen direct route goes down one of the steepest streets in Dunedin with a sharp bend. I could whip up a great speed pedalling hard in top gear until I could pedal no more, then I'd crouch down for aerodynamic effects. I reckon I was doing 70kph down towards Warrender Street and once I got around the sharp bend, I'd slam on the brakes for the final descent to George Street. It was pretty cool stuff. I even had an escape plan should the brakes fail, which was to roll up Queen Street, after the bend, until the bike stopped.

One day, I needed that escape plan. The brake-block composition materials were not great in the 1980s before mountain bikes came on the scene. That fateful day, it was raining and the road was streaming with water. Immediately after heading downhill, the brakes were having very little effect in the wet and my speed was slowly creeping up . . . I thought I'd better try to slow down by putting a foot on the road as another form of braking.

There was a lady in a car ahead of me slowing down for the sharp bend and there was me gaining on her with my heart in my mouth. Shit! Should I overtake her now? Will I get past her fast enough to get up Queen Street? Nah . . . too late . . . my front wheel was just a metre away from her bumper, my foot on the road spraying water up my leg, and I had a terrified look on my face.

The Queen Street exit was coming up so close . . . it was now or never! I squeezed past the car and slipped up the street until the bike stopped. Oh my god! My heart was beating hard and my legs were a little wobbly as I walked the bike down the rest of the hill.

Richard's passion for speed caught up with him when Ingrid got a complaint from a neighbour that her son was not only speeding, but had overtaken three cars on the way down the hill. Ingrid didn't mind her son having a bit of a wild streak, but Richard got a first warning.

Things became more serious when George caught him going down Pine Hill Road — the main route into Dunedin from the north — at 70kph. George 'punished' Richard by making him install a speedometer on the bike and vow to keep within the speed limits.

As a parenting decision, this didn't have the same effect as a piece of wood across the backside. It turned out George had completely misread his son's attitude to rule-breaking as Richard's goal soon became pushing the speedometer as far as it would go.

It didn't take much encouragement from Rob Smillie to test the limits — Rob had learned to drive and borrowed his mum's Mini so Richard could draught behind him and build speed downhill. One day, Richard managed to push his bike towards 75kph . . . a piece of information he never relayed to his father!

Towards the end of his high-school years, Richard and his friends took off on a cycling adventure that somewhat mirrored George's teenage excursion to Southland to photograph trains. The main difference was that Richard didn't go with the purpose of trainspotting, but his trip with Rob Smillie, and two of Rob's Otago Boys' High School mates, Angus Barclay and Les McNoe, was no less epic.

Rob's father Alistair loaded up the four boys' bikes on a trailer and drove them to Omarama, at the western end of the Waitaki Valley. From there the quartet rode over the Lindis Pass to Wanaka, where they bought a few beers and set up camp.

During the night, Les started throwing up and became so ill the others took him to the local doctor, who sent him off by ambulance to Dunedin Hospital. Richard can't remember the cause of the illness, but after they'd waved him off in the ambulance, Rob, Angus and Richard pushed on with their journey undeterred.

The next day involved a traverse of the Crown Range towards Queenstown. In those days, the road was unsealed and demanding, a jolting ride for novice touring cyclists on their thin-wheeled, light-framed, 10-speed bikes. They got part way — as far as where the Cardrona Distillery now sits — when an axle broke on Richard's bike. What to do? He decided to hitch a ride back to Wanaka where the group had left Les's bike. Richard took the axle from the abandoned bike, hitched a ride back up the Crown Range and put the new axle onto his bike.

Slowly, we got up Cardrona but, boy, were we stuffed. We were resting by the road at the top when a local farmer pulled up beside us and offered us a cold beer . . . We then had to go down the other side and, oh my god, that was frightening. The brake pads in those days were nowhere near as good as they are now and the gravel and dust just wore them out. The more we used the brakes, the hotter they got and the more worn down and less effective they became. Towards the bottom of the road, the rim of my wheel was too hot to touch.

Eventually, the trio cranked into Queenstown, exhausted, exhilarated and thirsty. A few too many beers preceded some poor attempts at chatting up a group of young women, and — as things do when teenagers and beer combine — an altercation broke out between Richard and another man.

It was near the waterfront in Queenstown and I must have told him to f-off or something. He punched me and my hearing aid flew off my ear and disappeared in the darkness. I was saying, "Fuck, you fucking wanker, I've lost my hearing aid!" and I was crawling around looking around for it.

He must have felt sorry for me as he stopped fighting and started helping me look for it. I got a torch, but that didn't help, we couldn't find it anywhere. I was devastated because hearing aids are so precious to me.

I got up the next morning and was determined to find it because the weather had changed and there were waves crashing over from Lake Wakatipu — I was thinking that if it's on the ground it will be wet and not working at all. But remarkably I found it! It was hanging on a branch in some bushes just above the ground. The battery had run down but it was still in good working order — it was a miracle!

From Queenstown, the crew rode along both the Kawarau and Cromwell gorges, down to Alexandra, through to the Maniototo — closely following the route of what is now the famed Otago Central Rail Trail — and on to Kokonga, where they camped by the river. The next morning, after just 14 kilometres of riding for the day, Rob Smillie snapped a crankshaft and, with no way to fix it, abandoned the ride at Hyde. He hitched a ride with an ice-cream delivery truck, putting his bike on the back and taking a ride all the way home to Dunedin. That left Richard and Angus, who in a bout of sheer bloody-mindedness decided to try to make it all the way home to Dunedin that day.

The hills between Middlemarch and Outram were quite devastating, so we did a lot of walking up the steep hills and then we'd get on the bikes and ride downhill. Finally, we got through to the Taieri Plains, but by the time we got to Three Mile Hill on the way into Dunedin, it was nearly nine o'clock at night and we'd left Kokonga at eight o'clock in the morning.

We were at the end of our tether and wondering if we'd make it up Three Mile Hill — but just as we were wondering if we'd make it home one of Angus's mates pulled up in a flat-deck truck and offered us a lift. We didn't have to think twice about getting a ride home!

CHAPTER

A MINI DIVERSION

When I was learning to drive, my mates tried to give me some tips. Grant Hanan had a Ford Prefect with just three forward gears and reverse. It was a bitch to try to drive and I kept stalling it, so Mum got me a driving instructor called Gareth Neville.

He took up the challenge of teaching a deaf person to drive in a manual car. He started off with him driving and me having my right hand on the gear lever, so I could feel the revs to get an idea of when it was time to change gears.

Richard's first car was a red Mini that had innumerable problems.

I couldn't hear the engine, but I could feel it and eventually I understood how the feel of the engine related to the revs and I could change gear with intuition. Gareth would use his hand to point whether I should turn left or right, as when I was driving I couldn't look at him to get instructions.

I passed my driving test and I was proud to have done that, but I didn't want to be reliant on driving Mum and Dad's car. A Mini appealed to me because Rob Smillie's parents had two of them.

I saw a Mini 850 advertised. It seemed to run clean, so I parted with my hard-earned cash and drove home that night. Mum said, 'Who brought you home?'

'Nobody.'

'How did you get home?'

'In the car.'

'Whose car?'

'My car.'

While not a petrol-head as such, Richard has always loved vehicles, though they haven't always loved him back. That original Mini proved an unmitigated disaster. The first lesson Richard learned about purchasing a car that's built low to the ground is to check under the carpet — like a lot of Minis, this one had developed a hole in the floor on the passenger side, which had been covered over with carpet. The driver's-side wheel arch also had an ominous soft spot where the rain got in. Then a crack appeared in the pillar of the driver's door, and one day the entire door handle came off.

The more I drove the car, the more faults I discovered. I should have picked them up before I bought it. One day I drove down Rattray Street and I was opposite Speight's brewery when 'Bang!' Suddenly, I couldn't see, so I stuck my head out the window to see where I was going and managed to pull over outside the brewery.

The bonnet had flipped open and blocked my view. What the hell? What was wrong? Whoops! It turned out the car had had so many modifications done to it the bonnet clip no longer worked — it had leather straps that I had forgotten to do up!

Another time, I was driving in a heavy rainstorm when I suddenly couldn't see any more. It was pissing down and the wiper was going so fast it just flew off so I had to pull over and hunt around on the road to find it and put it back on. Another time I went up to David Stedman's place and he took it for a drive up and down the street, and the next thing the whole exhaust pipe had fallen off. I put it in the back seat and drove around for a while without an exhaust pipe.

One day, when I slammed the door shut, the whole sliding window compartment fell into my lap. There were so many problems with that car.

Yet the car — which Stedman deduced had been in a roll-over accident — made it all the way to the North Island on one trip and, in the end, its demise came at the hands of Richard's driving.

The car lasted until I was practising my rally driving on a gravel road — I was trying to learn how to correct a slide and there was a patch where the gravel was laid quite thick.

The car slid off the road and hit a large rock. The impact staved in the passenger door. What's more, it was stuck on this rock and I couldn't get it off!

Eventually another car came along and we were able to push the Mini off the rock. I surveyed the damage, which was quite substantial, and my ego was pretty bruised as well.

I was thinking, 'How the hell am I going to explain this to Mum and Dad?' I had my pride to think about. And then I realised Mum and Dad's street was a narrow one-way and a neighbour's house had a wooden fence right on the road, so I could park the car hard against the fence and they wouldn't notice the dents.

I drove it around like that for two weeks — hiding the damage each night — trying to figure out what to do. Eventually I asked Grant Hanan if I could store it at his place while I placed an advertisement in the paper to sell it. Eventually,

Richard's second Mini was written off in an accident.

someone bought it and took it away and I even got some money for it.

When Mum asked where my car was I said, 'Oh, I sold it, I think it's time to move on to a proper car.'

They never knew what happened until I told them a few years later!

Richard's second Mini also ended its life in an accident, but not because of a fault with the car. This time Richard had learned a bit more about Minis and didn't make the same mistake of buying a lemon.

'One year, I took a holiday to Picton to follow a steam train that was coming down to Christchurch — it was around 1987 or 1988. I was working at Gregg's and I couldn't really afford a holiday but I wanted to photograph the train. So I took out the passenger seat and left it at home, then I put down a couple of beer crates, so I could sleep in the car. With my head on the back seat, I could just get my feet under the dashboard — it wasn't the most comfortable bed, but it was easier than taking a tent.'

Richard had some adventures 'hooning' around Dunedin. The Mini was small enough to drive across the St David Street pedestrian bridge at the heart of the university campus with a few centimetres to spare, and Richard took some pride in being able to get across the bridge without scraping the sides. 'You can't do that any more because they've put bollards in now.'

At one stage, Rob wanted to drive my car and we pulled up outside the 24-hour dairy to get some food. Then, for some reason, Rob decided to drive back up George Street along the footpath. Suddenly some blue flashing lights appeared.

The cop pulled us over and said, 'What gives you the right to drive on a footpath?'

Rob was muttering a few words while the police officer bent down to look across at me. He said, 'Oh, it's you.' It was my friend Phil Hurring's father, Bob.

Having recognised me, he asked us to explain why we were driving on the footpath. Rob made up a story that some bogans had been threatening us at the 24-hour dairy and we had to escape on the footpath.

Bob let us go with a warning — we were lucky to get away with that.

Richard liked the idea of learning to be a rally driver and often practised handbrake turns to spin the car or flip it around corners. 'I thought I was a good driver, but some people say I'm not.'

Determined to prove his skill, Richard entered a gymkhana at the

North Taieri gravel pit, home to the Dunedin Kart Club. The event entailed driving around several obstacles in the fastest time. To Richard's surprise — along with the car-club members' — he came third.

'Not bad for an amateur,' he said. 'I had my foot down the whole way and was doing handbrake turns. One of my classmates from primary school was in charge of the car club. It was a public open day and I thought I'd give it a go. It was good for my personal gratification.'

On one of the trips in his Mini, Richard picked up his first and last hitch-hiker.

I picked up this woman near Kaikoura — the roads were really windy and I said, 'Please don't talk to me when I'm driving because I can't turn my head to look at you.' But she wouldn't stop talking and I had to let her out at the first opportunity — I was quite relieved to get rid of her.

In later years, when rear-view mirrors got bigger, I was able to lip-read people in the mirror out of the corner of my eye. I can do it with people I know well, even if they are sitting in the back seat. I use my side mirrors more than most people in order to see what's behind me — that's what my driving instructor taught me — to keep looking.

Not hearing does bring its troubles on the road. Usually, Richard can hear ambulances and police car sirens, but not always as it depends on his

Richard's lifelong friend Rob Smillie.

Learning to drive was one of the more difficult tasks for Richard, as he had to be hyper-vigilant and couldn't hear his instructor.

Bottom: Long-time friend Grant Hanan.

surrounds. If there are a lot of tall buildings, they can block the sound. This was the case one day when Richard was crossing a one-way street near the university. He completely missed hearing a siren and crossed the road right in front of an ambulance, only narrowly missing a collision.

The car he was driving that day was not so lucky later in its life when Helen was driving it. She'd struck a deal with Richard that she could use the car if she paid some maintenance costs. She'd just put new tyres on it when she was collected by another car crossing one of Dunedin's one-way systems. While she was okay, Richard remembered the incident more for the fact numerous bottles of his home brew in the back of the car were smashed.

Later Emerson's Brewery had another Mini, known as the Mini Bar because it had a keg-pouring system installed in the back. The car could be driven, but it was usually taken from place to place on a trailer to save wear and tear. Richard's bad luck with Minis continued with that one when Emerson's sales and marketing manager Greg drove it up to Oamaru for an event. When he arrived he said, 'It's getting quite hot in there.' He'd forgotten to take the handbrake off . . . 'When we got it home the mechanic said the "brakes are fucked" and Greg was a little quiet about that one.'

The great thing about the Mini is that there's always a drama — it's not like these perfect, reliable Japanese cars. You always need to carry some CRC to clean the air filter and the engine doesn't start every time.

One day, I had real trouble getting it started outside my flat. The engine went for a second then it died. I pulled out the choke a bit, 'Vroom!', then it died. Pulled out the choke a bit more — same thing — it revved for a bit and then stopped. Finally, I revved it right up and it took off.

Later on at work, I went to get something out of the boot and I noticed there was some masking tape and a bit of rubber around the exhaust pipe. I couldn't work out what was going on.

When I got home that night, my flatmates were talking about putting potatoes in car exhaust pipes. They didn't get a response from me . . . eventually they had to explain it to me: that they had taped a condom onto the end of my exhaust pipe and had sat at the front window watching me rev it up.

Each time I turned the engine, the condom would inflate and come down . . . the back pressure was causing the car to stall. When I revved quite hard, the condom exploded with a big bang, but I never heard it so I just drove off not thinking anything of it. Meanwhile, they were inside pissing themselves laughing!

THE HOME-BREW BUG

In 1983, I had just finished high school and was at a crossroads in my life — my friends were going to university, but I wasn't sure what I wanted to do. Mum and Dad told me to give myself a break. I'd done two years of sixth form and high school was a difficult time for me — it really beat me up because I had to work hard to lip-read the teachers. I worked even harder on the internal assessment the second time around in sixth form and got accredited, but I was worn out.

Richard and colleagues from Cerebos Greggs.

George had earned a year's sabbatical in Edinburgh. Richard — just out of school and uncertain what direction his life would take or even what sort of career he'd like to pursue — ummed and ahhed about joining his parents and sister in Scotland.

The idea of staying in Dunedin and being fully independent from his parents, striking out on his own unencumbered, appealed to him, and in some ways it would prove to his parents that all the energy they'd put into equipping him for the world had been worth it.

But what would he do with himself for a year in Dunedin? Start studying? Burned out and exhausted from his repeat sixth-form year, that seemed a step too far.

He could stay home and find a job — not so easy for a deaf teen straight out of school. At almost 19, he considered manual labour as he was good with his hands and reckoned construction work or something similar would be okay. He'd enjoyed sciences at school but also had an artistic streak that he wanted to nurture. He could aim higher. In short, he stood in limbo, not certain what the next step should be, not knowing where his true capabilities lay.

'WE COULDN'T LEAVE HIM STRUGGLING AT HOME,' INGRID SAID, 'SO WE SAID, "COME WITH US TO EDINBURGH." AND THAT'S WHERE HE FOUND BEER.'

His eventual decision put the rest of his life in motion. 'We couldn't leave him struggling at home,' Ingrid said, 'so we said, "Come with us to Edinburgh." And that's where he found beer.'

Armed with a new camera and with a gap year ahead of him, Richard hit the famous streets of Edinburgh with ambition, surprising his parents with his ability to comfortably navigate the city within a couple of days of their arrival.

He approached a polytech in the city and asked about enrolling in a science course. The time frame didn't work, but they directed him to an arts programme where he enrolled in a drawing and photography course.

He also took himself off to find the local Boys' Brigade and asked if he could be of assistance. Boys' Brigade had been an important element of his childhood, providing camaraderie, discipline and independence. Before long, it served the same purpose for him in Edinburgh, introducing him to the pub scene, thanks to the group's older members, who took him to their favourite local watering holes.

I appreciated the British pubs — they were places to go and talk, socialise, play pool — and then I discovered the beers. So different to New Zealand. They had much more flavour and were not so fizzy. I said to myself, 'Hell, what are we drinking back in New Zealand?' It was almost devoid of flavour compared with the beer in Scotland.

The pubs were a social gathering place — you met people in the pub — it was the opposite of New Zealand with its Friday-night binge-drinking culture. The beer was better and was served in pint glasses — that was civilisation!

Some of the pubs were lovely old things, with beautiful woodwork and ceramic tiles. It was paradise. The experience stayed with me and when I started Emerson's Brewery, I did it with a determination to cultivate our drinking here in New Zealand — drinking less but better.

The sabbatical proved important for George as well. Helen Emerson noted that while her father loved whisky, beer rarely made its way into the Emerson house unless George had to host a train society meeting and would buy a crate.

Richard's discovery of a real ale aligned with George working at the biological sciences department at Heriot-Watt University, where brewing and distilling had been taught since 1903 and where the chemistry department gave lectures on brewing. So ingrained is the subject that, in 1988, the renowned International Centre for Brewing and Distilling opened as a stand-alone unit inside the Heriot-Watt's biological sciences department.

In that regard, Edinburgh didn't change George's life as much as it did Richard's, but the emphasis Heriot-Watt put on brewing elevated the noble science in George's thinking.

Helen Emerson's memory of Edinburgh as a 12-year-old captured the sense of change in the air: 'It felt like an important time for the family.'

The fact that Richard took a course in photography strengthened the bond between him and George. Helen believed Richard had a calling for photography and other visual arts. He had an extraordinary eye for detail and an almost photographic memory; partly because sound didn't distract him and partly because he had to rely on his visual awareness to compensate for his hearing loss.

While he had an artist's eye for framing a photograph and had become adept at sketches and line drawings, he also brought his intense focus to the task.

'He's always been obsessive and methodical,' Helen said. 'And with photography it was no different. He carried pocket notebooks and for every photo he took he would write down the exposure, the f-stop . . . all the details of the particular photo. Then when he got slides processed, he could go back and check his settings to see what had given the best results.'

That methodical nature was something Richard had learned from his father. Throughout his life, George took more than 10,000 photographs — mostly of trains. Each negative and colour slide in his collection was dated and its location noted.

When I got home from Scotland in 1984, I was at another crossroads. I'd done fine arts in Edinburgh and I was trying to decide whether to become an artist or a scientist, and whether to study or find work.

I decided to go to Otago Polytechnic to study for a New Zealand Certificate of Science in order to become a laboratory technician. I felt I wasn't cut out to go to university to become a scientist, but as a laboratory technician I could make good use of my science study at high school.

I also decided I needed a job. There was a possibility of a job in the anatomy department at Otago University, but that didn't eventuate. I was looking at the newspaper every day, searching for jobs, and I applied for a lot of them. The only place that even offered me an interview was Cerebos Gregg's. I got that job working in the food science lab.

Mum and Dad weren't impressed that I wasn't concentrating on my study, but hey, jobs like this don't come up very often. It was quite a struggle for me to study and cope with the rigours of full-time work. But I got through and got my qualifications and I did it on my own, making Mum and Dad proud of me. Not only that, but I also moved into a flat to be truly independent.

If ever a career could bridge Richard's indecision between art and science it was brewing — he just didn't know it at that point. He took the job at Cerebos Gregg's having learned that interviews — let alone jobs — came along rarely. It may have been his only choice, but the position perfectly suited his future need. It seems fated especially as his short time at Gregg's coincided with the brief few years the company produced malt extract at its Forth Street factory.

The timing proved critical for Richard's success as a brewer — the job gave him access to malt extract and, later, wort (the unfermented beer used to make the extract). Talk about serendipity!

Cerebos, the global food giant, merged with established Dunedin business Gregg's in 1985 to form Cerebos Gregg's. Gregg's had long been associated with the production of Maltexo malt extract, which they made at the nearby Wilson whisky distillery. After Seagram's bought Wilson Distillers, the malt extract production continued in a leased space at the distillery. Following the merger with Cerebos, production moved to the main Gregg's site where Richard worked.

Despite his involvement in the production of malt extract — commonly used in home brew — brewing his own beer hadn't yet occurred to Richard. His good friend David Stedman had taken up the role of home brewer. 'I was making home brew with Maltexo, sugar and brewer's yeast — it was all

Richard's passion for beer quickly turned into an obsession.

you could get. I kept doing it that way, all the while hoping the next brew would miraculously be better than the last.'

Richard tried to help David improve his brewing by sourcing ingredients slightly better than those off the supermarket shelf, but even then it took a twist of fate for Richard's mind to open to brewing himself.

I was quite envious of David because he was making home brew. We were always talking about and enjoying beer. But this one day I went over and he was capping bottles with the old-style hammer capper. Just as I walked in, he hit the cap and the entire side of the bottle broke away and beer came pouring out. Something happened in my mind at that moment and I thought, 'I can do better than that.'

'That incident turned a light on for him,' Stedman recalled. 'I think it [brewing] would have happened at some stage, but he saw me making a hash of it and thought, "This looks like fun and I bet I can do it better than David." '

Richard made his first home brew in Ingrid's kitchen on 27 August 1985, recording the experiment in a notebook he's kept for over 30 years.

According to his notes, the recipe came from *Home Winemakers Recipes*, which Richard found in the library at Gregg's. The book was written by local man David McKechie, who was a member of the Dunedin Amateur Winemakers and Brewers Club in the 1970s.

The recipe required a can of malt extract, 250 grams of sugar and 30 grams of hops. He used a tin of malt extract, rough old hops (unlikely to be fresh) and a packet of DYC yeast (also likely to be at the rank end of the flavour spectrum). After boiling for an hour and allowing it to cool overnight, Richard added the yeast the next morning. All up, he made 4.5 litres of beer, enough for six 750ml bottles.

His tasting notes suggest the beer had a good head, but tasted too bitter. The overall flavour passed muster. As a rudimentary start, he found enough positives to keep him interested. As any home brewer will attest, if the first brew turns out to be half-decent, it's usually enough to kick-start the obsession.

The tasting notes for a second brew were less detailed, but equally telling, with the words 'weasel piss' scrawled across the page of his notebook!

Undeterred by that effort, Richard pressed on. The process appealed to his meticulous, scientific approach, the tasting talked to his love of

flavours and with every beer that proved drinkable he went deeper down the rabbit hole. On top of everything else, he and George bonded over the 'quality control'.

Richard's attuned taste buds knew the flavour could be better. George had some knowledge of yeast, so that became the first element Richard played around with, trying different yeasts to see how they might change the flavour profile of his beer. For a wannabe home brewer, it's hard to overstate the importance of yeast and Richard was blessed to have a father with the requisite skills in handling and cultivating it.

Richard also knew that he could get better flavour by brewing with real grain rather than malt extract, and his job at Cerebos Gregg's offered a huge benefit in that regard thanks to their Ward Street malthouse, where they malted grain for Maltexo.

Richard loved visiting the malthouse, likening the smell of germinating barley to fresh cucumber. There, he acquired small amounts of fresh grain,

A rare family portrait.

which allowed him to move to the elite level of home brewing known as all-grain brewing.

With a rudimentary knowledge of the process, Richard crushed the malt in the laboratory at work. He then soaked it in warm water to extract the sweet maltose from the grain, a process known as mashing.

Without the right equipment, this is a complex task, and it's fair to say Richard's initial attempts at 'running off' the liquid that would turn into beer proved disastrous. 'Initially I tried straining it through a tea towel, but that made a hell of a mess all over my mother's kitchen. Eventually I used a fine sieve and, while it was still messy, I was getting clear wort and I knew I was getting somewhere.'

He likened the difference between brewing with malt extract and grain to the difference between using instant coffee versus using whole beans. The flavour changed dramatically.

It wasn't long before Richard's obsessive and methodical personality applied itself to the task of making better beer. Not content to make around 23 litres at a time in his mother's kitchen, Richard ramped up production, making up to 120 litres at a time, which he would sometimes divide into five batches, fermenting each one with a different strain of yeast. Naturally, Ingrid's kitchen couldn't handle this level of production and Richard convinced a friend to let him brew in an empty double garage in Ravensbourne.

At this point, David — despite Richard's help in supplying materials — stopped brewing. 'There was no point any more because Richard was doing it too well. He'd taken it to another level.'

Instead, Stedman became Richard's black-market agent, distributing crates of home brew for 'donations' of around $15 each. The money went back to Richard to reinvest in ingredients and equipment. The drinkers — or 'appreciators' as Richard and David called them — also had an obligation to critique the beer. Each bottle came marked with a number on the cap, which Richard cross-referenced on an index so any feedback could be recorded. Any brews not up to scratch got biffed, so the bottles could be reused in the next batch.

Stedman knew Richard had created something magical, that alchemy was unfolding before them. 'You couldn't buy this beer anywhere else and people knew it was good and they wanted it — slowly there was this culture shift happening; Richard was getting people to change their drinking habits.'

He also realised that the beer was destined for commercial success when a friend and budding businessman, John Devereux, offered to buy everything David could get his hands on. 'John was pretty shrewd and I knew that if he wanted more, I was on to a good thing.'

Richard's home-brew enterprise could easily have tipped into a professional microbrewery that wouldn't have been out of place in the New Zealand scene as it stood in the late eighties. In fact, his system was more sophisticated than many professional outfits of the time. The work involved in what was largely a hobby back then laid the groundwork for a fledgling brewery. To bottle and cap each 120-litre batch required 15 dozen 750ml bottles and many hours of devoted focus. Once bottled, the beer had to be stored upright for three or four weeks in order for it to condition. At one stage, Richard had 120 dozen bottles of beer on the go — either conditioning or out in the world being 'appreciated'.

HE LIKENED THE DIFFERENCE BETWEEN BREWING WITH MALT EXTRACT AND GRAIN TO THE DIFFERENCE BETWEEN USING INSTANT COFFEE VERSUS USING WHOLE BEANS. THE FLAVOUR CHANGED DRAMATICALLY.

Besides being a malt source, Gregg's also provided Richard with access to a large library full of books on food, wine and beer. In those pre-internet days, beer information proved elusive, so getting access to this kind of material helped Richard's enterprise to reach a whole new level. He read anything he could get his hands on and learned not only how to make beer, but also how to make the equipment he needed.

In 1980s New Zealand — as many other beer pioneers discovered — small-scale brewing equipment didn't exist, so many start-up microbreweries used converted dairy equipment to make their beer.

Richard learned to make his own equipment, creating approximations of what he'd seen in books. He quickly worked out how to improvise solutions when what he needed wasn't readily available, something he'd learned from building the model railway in the family basement.

He also benefited from the connections that come with living in a small city. Avid home brewer Ken Logan worked at the Wilson distillery, and he gifted Richard a yeast culture — heritage uncertain — which became the house yeast when Emerson's Brewery started.

There are thousands of yeast strains in the brewing world and many established breweries closely guard their yeasts because they can be such a defining character in the finished product. Logan thought his yeast had come from either Harley's brewery in Nelson, long since defunct, or possibly from somewhere in Denmark, which given Richard's heritage on his mother's side seems a better story.

Regardless of where it came from, Richard kept this yeast culture going for years, and it became the workhorse that fermented most of his early beers.

I called it my KL strain after Ken. That yeast had the best flavour and it became our house strain of yeast. Ken knew my father — Dunedin being a small town you got to know people but Dad also made connections through the biochemistry department.

Dad loved beer. It was good coming home from the brewery, bringing home some beers, and we'd talk about the flavours and he'd fall asleep. He was never a big beer drinker, but he was interested in the flavours and keen to support me in what I was doing.

In the late 1980s, Richard had a good life — he was making beer, earning a nice living at Cerebos Gregg's and piggybacking on the company's wealth of knowledge while getting access to ingredients other home brewers could only dream about.

Looking back, he had an inkling it would be 'quite cool to set up a brewery', but he didn't have the spark, the motivation, needed to launch a business while he enjoyed paid employment and easy access to everything needed for his large-scale home-brew enterprise. He needed a jolt to take him out of his comfort zone. That came in 1990 with the news that Cerebos Gregg's had been sold to Japanese food giant Suntory.

Along with 89 others in Dunedin, Richard faced redundancy. The process took a long time to play out because of a dispute over the redundancy offer, with remaining workers at Cerebos Gregg's in Dunedin as well as staff in Auckland going on strike over the initial offer of six weeks' pay. The company settled the dispute by raising its offer to 12 weeks' pay for the first year of service and two weeks' pay for each subsequent year.

As Richard remembers it, the laid-off workers spent weeks in limbo as the dispute played out — they knew they'd be out the door one day, but they had no idea when. In the meantime they came to work with little incentive to do anything. Richard, effectively laid off and waiting for a payout, did what came naturally: he made beer.

I had to wait for a long time to get my redundancy cheque, but there was no work to do. I was being paid to make home brew in the lab. At around 3.30pm or 4pm I'd break out the home brews and everyone came to help me test them. As we got closer to being laid off the drinking started at three o'clock.

Other days at 4.30pm, I started in the factory packing spices at time-and-a-half — there was plenty of casual work because they had laid off too many people. So, I went to work all day getting paid for reading the paper, drinking coffee and brewing, and then I'd work in the evening at time-and-a-half!

The redundancy offered Richard a chance to rethink his career path. He knew how hard it had been to get a job in the first place and realised that another great job wouldn't come so easily — especially as New Zealand's unemployment rate pushed towards double digits.

A brewing dream took on an abstract shape, but Richard — being the scrupulous researcher, the meticulous investigator of options — decided he needed to find out a bit more about brewing and beer.

Hello Grandma,
Sorry for not keeping in contact with you since I've been told I was being made redundant from work. This really turned my world upside down, in fact, it gave me the chance to travel overseas. Uncle Richard was good in getting me a job in the brewery so I can see at hand what they do and what cleaning methods they use. I still want to run a brewpub one day as a family enterprise with a restaurant. But I'll have to look into it very carefully. I want to keep it small and manageable as well

as being within financial grasp. I was very sad to hear of Pop's passing. Ingrid was most upset and rang me at work. After Perth, I'm going to Europe and the UK and the USA. At the moment I'm toying with the idea of visiting Russia now that it's all 'open'. It's good to hear you are now feeling stronger and in good health as well as keeping in touch with Ingrid over the phone. Will keep you posted.

Love Richard

—Postcard to Grandma Holst, 15 February 1990

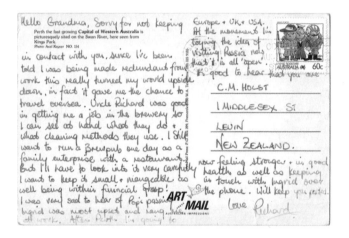

Fate, eh? There might not have been an exact moment when Richard Emerson knew he wanted to be a brewer. The calling presented itself through a series of moments when the planets aligned for him in so many ways — from the trip to Edinburgh as an impressionable 18-year-old, to seeing David Stedman make a hash of home brewing, to getting a job at a place that made malt, to having a biochemist father — even being born stone deaf somehow funnelled him in that direction by closing off so many other options. Whether his acute sense of taste and love of food came naturally or whether he had to develop it in a compensatory sense is a subject for endless discussion. Either way, he had a palate that set him apart from most others.

So not one moment but a series of moments added up to a pre-determined outcome — and yet at some point he had to articulate it, and that postcard to his grandmother from Perth in February 1990 carries the essence of that plan. Somehow it reinforces the whole idea that by putting something in writing, by stating the dream, you can make it all come true.

The small steps, the building blocks, continued to fall in a pattern that's obvious when viewed in retrospect. The 'Uncle Richard' in the postcard is Ingrid's brother, Richard Holst, a zoologist who'd moved to Perth. He had connections at Fremantle's Matilda Bay Brewing Company — one of the early independent breweries in Australia's craft beer renaissance. Richard Emerson had offered to work there for nothing just to learn the ropes, but they offered him paid work so he packed his bag, including his 'bible' — Michael Jackson's *Pocket Guide to Beer* — and set off for an adventure.

Before he left, he had the small problem of where to store 120 crates of home brew, which would continue to find their way into the hands of the appreciators in his absence. Figuring out how to transport so many crates of beer in his tiny Mini was another IQ-stretching problem for Richard.

I had well over 120 swappa crates — it was a bit of a problem when I had to move them out of the Ravensbourne garage in the Mini. The passenger seat had only two nuts and bolts, so if I took the passenger seat out I was able to get 15 crates in there and that's how I moved all my home brew to a basement belonging to neighbours of my parents.

When I got back from overseas, Dad gave me a glass of beer that was beautifully clear and flavoursome. 'Dad,' I said, 'why are you giving me Duvel [a famous Belgian beer]?'

'It's not Duvel,' he said, 'it's your beer.'

'No, it's not.'

And then he showed me the crown cap number and I thought, 'Oh my god, that's the best beer I've ever made and I threw most of it out.' You see, I used to sample the beer as I brewed it and if a batch was no good I would tip it out to free up bottles for the next brew. In that brew, I'd dumped all but two dozen because I thought it wasn't very good.

It's a shame it took a year of storing to get that good and I said to Dad: 'It's great but it's not a very economical beer to make if you have to store it so long.'

When Richard arrived in Western Australia, he found Matilda Bay to be a massive brewery, churning out 20,000-litre batches, round the clock, six days a week. It gave him invaluable knowledge of all the arcane stuff required to make beer on a large scale — cleaning systems, how pumps worked, the types of tanks required — but he left there sooner than expected after his disability was held against him for the first time in his life.

At Matilda Bay, I was a labourer doing a lot of cleaning. I didn't learn about making beers, but how to use the pumps, move the hoses, clean the tanks. I was there for about four months. I'd had enough at Matilda Bay after an argument with my boss over being late. I'd go to work by train, and one day I was late to work because the train broke down.

Another day, my train didn't break down, but the one in front of it did! So, I was late to work again. We didn't have mobile phones in those days and I couldn't have called in anyway — what could I do? My boss was ranting at me and I said, 'I'm quitting.' I wasn't happy with how I was treated because I had no way of telling them I was running late — I didn't think that was right.

From Perth, he headed to Britain. Guided by Michael Jackson's book, his first port of call was the famous 300-year-old pub, The Lamb. 'I had a Young's Special bitter. I was hanging out to make my first beer in London a real ale.'

In London, Richard briefly found work as an orderly in an operating theatre, which allowed him to save up enough money to travel Europe by rail. There Jackson's well-thumbed bible led him to famous beers and breweries in Germany and Belgium.

On this journey of discovery, Richard took careful notes and memorised flavour profiles. 'I wanted to taste the beers in their home towns, and with Michael Jackson's book I learned to analyse the flavours of different beer styles.'

Back in London, he'd read about a brewing course in Yorkshire. He'd tried without luck to pick up a job in a brewery, so enrolling in the course seemed the best way to gain knowledge of traditional real ale brewing methods.

Travelling there by train from London was half the fun. I took the HST [high speed train] from London to York, then a little DMU [Diesel Multiple Unit] from York to a country town, Malton, where I stayed at the pub. The brewing course was at the back of the pub. The information was relatively simple, most of the things I already knew from working at Matilda Bay, but it was good to get a feeling for the British brewing industry.

The highlight of the course was a bus trip to the famous Samuel Smith Old Brewery in Tadcaster. This is one of Yorkshire's oldest breweries and one of the few still using huge slate Yorkshire fermentation squares.

Walking into the room full of stone squares, the walls over five centimetres thick, remains one of my highlights of the trip. It was an incredible sight to see thick, creamy yeast-head alive, in motion, with bubbles popping. I doubt if I would get to see such a spectacle again in this new era of health and safety.

Having a few pints at the pub attached to the brewery was a real enjoyment; pints of rich, creamy, fruity ales went down a real treat! I have huge respect for Samuel Smith ales, having drunk a fair few pints. This wonderful ale would have a fight for the customer's attention nowadays as the hoppy beers have secured a strong hold on the beer drinkers' tongue.

Richard returned to Dunedin after his year away determined to make a career in brewing. He knew how hard it had been for him to get his first job at Cerebos Gregg's, and while he didn't see his deafness as an obstacle, his experience in Perth made him wise to the fact that others could see it as such. On top of that, he returned to a country in an economic crisis, with unemployment soaring and only a limited range of work suitable to a profoundly deaf young man.

I knew it would be more than difficult to get a job — mainly because I can't use a telephone. The range of work for me would have been quite narrow compared with other people. It wasn't easy in that regard. I know one other deaf person who has managed to do well — he is not as deaf as I am and he can use a telephone. I would have been okay as a builder but not a painter — I couldn't paint and talk to people.

UP AND RUNNING ... ON EMPTY

Dad had talked to a property developer who was thinking of setting up a microbrewery in the university area. That fell through, but George was convinced it was a good idea. Dad thought he could help me make it happen. He was fully behind it. He said to me, 'If you think you can do this I will get some shareholders together and we'll set up a company.' So I spent the next two years developing a business plan and getting equipment.

Richard says a small prayer as he sets up his first brewery at 4 Grange Street, Dunedin.

I would travel up to Christchurch a lot to look at the breweries up there — the Loaded Hog was one of them — they didn't want people to know how they succeeded, but I read between the lines.

We couldn't afford to be flash when we set up the plant. He had an inkling there were others getting into the microbrewing business, but Dad knew his beers, and he was sure there was a place for the porter we had in mind to brew.

Ingrid Emerson has a clear recollection of the first time she heard talk of a brewery spoken aloud — or rather shouted — in the house. In the late 1990s, home from his travels, Richard knew what he wanted.

'Richard came storming in one night and rushed up to George's study, and the noise that came after that . . . I didn't hear what was said initially, but the next thing was a shriek from the study. It was George shouting, "You want what?"

"I want a brewery," came Richard's reply.

"Well, we haven't got the money for a brewery!"'

After a few more heated words, the pair calmed down and George told his son: 'You'll have to go and develop a plan for what you want to do and how you're going to do it, talk to publicans around town and see if they want your beer, and work out how you will get it to them. Then come back to me.'

This was typical of George — gruff, frugal, curmudgeonly — but deep down, he'd become enamoured with the idea of Richard as a brewer. He'd drunk the home brew, and he knew it was good. He saw obsession, passion, determination. He knew brewing could suit his son. Communication wouldn't be as critical as in other jobs — or so he thought. He'd always worried about his son finding a suitably engaging career, and he could see that Richard running a successful business might be just the ticket. But his son had always been headstrong — forever going too fast — and he needed to apply the brakes, check the speedometer, put a reality leash on Richard's unrestrained enthusiasm.

George loved the role of 'action man', as his railway friend Bill Cowan described him. He got things done. While Richard researched the market demand for microbrewed beer in Dunedin, George looked at ways to make the concept a reality. He approached the project in the same way he'd done with the Otago Excursion Train Trust, but his volunteers weren't restoring railway carriages in their free time, instead they were 'volunteering' cash for start-up capital.

As Rob Smillie recalled, the venture had an element of George riding shotgun on Richard's dream. 'The idea of doing this brewery thing appealed to him. He wasn't approaching retirement by any means, but he wanted to do something different. He and Graeme Berry [a railway mate of George's] had the idea of doing this and they approached our family — Mum and Dad and me.'

Richard and George developed a business plan, working out they'd need roughly $100,000 of start-up capital to lease space, buy equipment and ingredients, and pay Richard a salary of $15,000 a year — a fraction over the minimum wage at the time.

———

HE SAW OBSESSION, PASSION, DETERMINATION. HE KNEW BREWING COULD SUIT HIS SON. COMMUNICATION WOULDN'T BE AS CRITICAL AS IN OTHER JOBS — OR SO HE THOUGHT.

———

George did all the fundraising — the bulk of the capital came from him and Ingrid — but family friends chipped in, as did biochemistry colleagues and George's fellow railway enthusiasts. Graeme Berry made the second-highest contribution. Richard's two lifelong friends, Rob Smillie and Grant Hanan, put in money, as did Smillie's parents Alistair and Shirley, and the parents of another friend, Paul Trotman. His famous aunt Alison Holst and her husband Peter and Richard's uncle Les all contributed.

Bizarrely — or perhaps ironically — some of the seed money for Emerson's came from Lion Breweries, or Lion Nathan as it was then. Richard's great-aunt had bought shares in Lion's predecessor, New Zealand Breweries, and they had been held in an Emerson family trust after her passing. With the agreement of the relevant family members, the trust sold the shares to raise capital for Richard's brewery.

Ingrid and George wanted to put in more money than their $24,000, but couldn't afford it. Richard had $1000 to invest and the rest of the 13 original investors put down between $2500 and $7000 each, making a grand total of $93,000.

Many of the original shareholders felt like they'd given to charity — in all honesty they figured they'd never see that money again. Ingrid candidly admitted that some might have 'donated' in sympathy 'to help their friends with the deaf son'.

Grant Hanan, who'd known Richard since the pair were six-year-olds at Maori Hill School, put in $5000 in combination with his brother and sister. Looking back, it seemed like a lot of money to invest in a friend's fledgling business. In a sector dominated by two giant breweries success was not a given, but Grant believed in Richard — he'd tasted the beer, knew it was good.

'I'd go around to my parents' place and do tasting sessions — leading up to the company formation there had been a lot of experimentation — and we knew the beer was good. The investment wasn't taken lightly but I could see the quality was there. The only real competitor in terms of independent beer was Mac's, and I thought Richard's beer was better than what they were putting out. We knew the quality was there, but getting the market to appreciate it was the gamble.

'I had spent time in England where my grandfather was a member of CAMRA [Campaign for Real Ale], so I knew an alternative beer scene existed and had potential. It hadn't taken off in New Zealand but people were sick of what was on offer, so they'd started drinking imported beer like Beck's because it was something different.

'I was prepared to give him a chance. It just seemed like a natural thing to do — and anyway I'd probably drunk $5000 worth of his beer before I made the commitment! I had a lot of faith in Richard's ability. He was driven and had energy to burn, especially in those days. He was also physically strong — he could carry three crates of beer without trouble and he wasn't shy of hard work. I knew he could push himself physically.'

While George went around cap in hand, Richard signed on for the dole and spent 18 months perfecting his brewing technique — he'd become enamoured with a recipe for porter that he'd picked up in London and his appreciators thought it was fantastic.

Richard collected his welfare cheque every Thursday, as did thousands of other New Zealanders, with unemployment peaking at 10.7 per cent in 1992. Thankfully, the welfare system had adapted somewhat over the

'I HAD A LOT OF FAITH IN RICHARD'S ABILITY. HE WAS DRIVEN AND HAD ENERGY TO BURN, ESPECIALLY IN THOSE DAYS. HE WAS ALSO PHYSICALLY STRONG — HE COULD CARRY THREE CRATES OF BEER WITHOUT TROUBLE AND HE WASN'T SHY OF HARD WORK. I KNEW HE COULD PUSH HIMSELF PHYSICALLY.'

years and it allowed Richard to keep drawing the dole while he started his one-man business — making his benefit a type of self-employment start-up payment, which proved helpful because the business didn't have enough to pay him a wage.

Apart from hardware, Emerson's invested in a unique logo. Again George's contacts came in handy as one of his friends, John Swan, owned T&D Advertising in Dunedin. Richard worked with the company's creatives and together they created a hand-drawn font reflecting Emerson's classic style.

Emerson's Brewing Company Ltd came into existence in October 1992 and took up the lease on an old shoe warehouse at 4 Grange Street, Dunedin. Richard spent the spring of 1992 putting in a wet floor — a raised concrete floor with self-contained drainage — painting, and getting equipment fabricated at Dunedin engineering firm Farra Engineering.

I wanted to do business with a local company because it's better for me to have face-to-face contact. I couldn't have done that with someone overseas. I had to pay a little bit more, but I got quality and it worked straight away.

I did make mistakes — we had a wee extractor fan that I thought would do the job, but when I did the first brew there was steam everywhere, I couldn't see a thing, so we had to spend a bit more money on that. I was lucky to have people we knew who were good enough to help us.

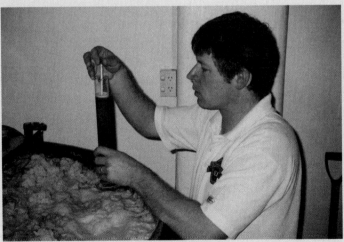

Richard loved cask ales, and his early batches of beer were served from wooden casks handmade in Christchurch.

In the early 1990s, craft beer — that catch-all descriptor and the boom industry attached to it — didn't exist in this country. In fact, it was still 15 or 20 years away. At the time, microbrewery was a vogue term for a mainstream alternative, a way of differentiating small, handmade products from the mass-produced beer churned out by Lion and DB.

Until Emerson's came along with their emphasis on flavour and classical styles, sorting breweries by size became the simplest way to separate the ruling duopoly from small upstarts that followed the establishment of Mac's by Terry McCashin in Nelson in 1981.

In reality, apart from size (and quality), the difference between big and small in the 1980s was minimal in terms of the type of beer they made. Many of the new breed of brewers did little more than create handmade versions of the big-boy beers. They followed an established pattern of creating three products — colloquially known as yellow, amber and black, aka lager, amber ale and dark beer (which was usually just a dark lager).

"I GRADUALLY EASED OUT THE BUNG AND SUDDENLY IT EXPLODED. THE BUNG FLEW OUT OF MY HAND, HIT THE CEILING LIKE A BULLET AND BOUNCED AROUND THREE WALLS. THERE WAS A GEYSER OF BEER ABOUT A METRE AND A HALF HIGH."

This microbrewery mirroring of the mass market was a result of the ingredients to make anything more exotic not being available. The big breweries set the market parameters and the niche brewers remained too small to create change. Besides which, a quantum leap in flavour would have been too much for a novice market to handle. Even if there had been a demand for different beers, most brewers in the country at the time lacked the knowledge to make alternative styles. All of this meant that from the get-go Richard Emerson had started a very unusual brewery.

Richard had deep knowledge; he'd perfected a wide range of styles as a home brewer. Plus, he'd tested the underground market for years, so he knew that if he made something different, there would be a small audience for it.

Not content to do one or two things differently, Richard took a huge leap of faith by doing three things that were completely unexpected. He came to market with his London Porter, a beer style brought back from the edge of extinction; a cloudy, tart German wheat beer; and an English-style bitter. He created an array of styles barely heard of in this country and well outside people's taste expectations. He then put them in 500ml plastic bottles — a container no one had seen or used in the Kiwi beer market — and, most contrarily, he sold his beer to pubs in 30-litre wooden casks.

Back then, breweries had only just stopped trucking beer in large tankers and pumping it into large underground vats. The beer scene resembled Rip van Winkle, rubbing his eyes after waking up from a long sleepwalk through the era of the six o'clock swill. It's easy to imagine how bar managers would have baulked at the sight of this young man walking in with a 30-litre wooden cask — they didn't know what to do with such a thing. And among drinkers, glass bottles were either staunchly 750ml — usually purchased via the swap-a-crate system — or in six- or 12-packs of 330ml bottles or cans. Plastic and 500ml? Those two concepts were nowhere on drinkers' radars.

Dad had connections at Ferrymead Heritage Park in Christchurch where there was a cooper working. A guy called David Bain. He was at pains to emphasise his name was David P. Bain to differentiate from the other, at that time, more notorious David Bain!

David built us 30-litre barrels. He had made 20-litre pins for Speight's brewery, but I wanted a bigger size than that. He made two prototypes, which I played with — one was a 50-litre one I called the Big Mother and the other was 30 litres called Slim Jim because it was long and narrow.

With the 50-litre barrel I was trying to cask condition — I racked off the beer into the barrel and put a rubber bung in the top. A couple of days later, I went back and could see beer seeping through the grain at the end of the barrel. I thought, 'Oh, there's a little bit too much pressure, so I better relieve it.' I gradually eased out the bung and suddenly it exploded. The bung flew out of my hand, hit the ceiling like a bullet and bounced around three walls. There was a geyser of beer about a metre and a half high. I was trying to stop it with my hand,

PXE 15PR 1 45   55,000

/   EMERSON'S BREWING Co. LTD.

15ᵗʰ JAN 1993.

BREW No. 01

HWT TEMP   78.8°C

Planned mashing postponed to later due to
presence of thermal layer in HWT. Water in
mash foundation only 45-50°C.
Switched off clock (in HWT) returned H₂O back.
Reheat.

   8.05 am   71°C   Nights rate. begin 17.6
                                                finish 31.0

* 9.15 am   80°C ⓦ circulation

                              Day Rate. begin 41.2
Mash temp   66°C   78gm CaCO₃ in Mash.
Mash stand 10.15 am. Start Mashing in 9.20 am

Start Sparge + Runoff 12.00 pm.   1 x 18l Return

1.20pm   Elements on Full. BUZZER ON
2.35pm.   WORT GRAVITY   CONTINUOUSLY
             1100   OG = 1040°   WHY?
             .250   1375l.
             600

                                         850
       Boil 4.30pm.   150   450
1ˢᵗ. Hops 4.40pm. 850gm. Super A. 1000   200
2ⁿᵈ.   5.20   150 200gm Super A.   —
3ʳᵈ   5.45pm. 600gm Hallertau.   650
                                          200
                                        850

The handwritten log of the first two brew days at 4 Grange Street.

Brew #02.   5. Feb 1993.

84.8% 220 kg	Pale Malt.	Water treatment.
10.48% 27.2	Crystal.	= 80gm $CaCO_3$.
4.7 12.2	Roast Malt.	
259.4		

Liquor temp = 85.5°C

Mash Temp 67°C   Mash Stand 8.50am.
                    end Mash.   10.20am.

1st liquor used 450l.
    remain 1340l.   Wort = 1450.

                                    80mins
Power on 1.30pm.   1st HOPS 3.40   900 gm
Boil   3.30pm.
                                 4.20pm. 200gm.
Finish   5.00pm.
                                 4.45   650
    Boiled wort 1410l.

Pump thru Paraflow 30mins.
Still to hot, cool @ jackets.

LONDON PORTER

London Porter was the first beer produced by Emerson's. It was based on a recipe Richard picked up at a brewpub in London, The Orange. His version of the recipe has evolved over the years but the beer has remained a stalwart of the New Zealand craft scene for over a quarter-century.

For the uninitiated: there's a lovely chocolate aroma and roast grain character similar to wholegrain bread that's spent a fraction too long in the toaster but is not yet burnt. The body is light and easy going, belying the deep ruby colour, but it finishes firm and dry. It was a gamble to start

his brewing empire with a dark beer, but Richard wanted a beer that would serve well from a traditional cask, plus he saw a gap in the market as at that time there were not many dark beers being made by the big breweries.

but beer was just spraying everywhere — I was soaked — there was nothing I could do, but let it go and I lost about 15 litres. I was drenched and smelling of beer. I couldn't believe how much pressure that barrel could hold — and that the bung was so tight the beer was going out through the grain.

That wasn't the reason I went for the 30-litre barrel — it was because the 50-litre one was far too heavy to lift. The weight of the wood and the beer was too much for my back. The 30-litre barrel weighed about the same as a 50-litre stainless steel keg. I wanted the wooden barrels for the romanticism of it and as a point of difference. They looked cute with the Emerson's name on the side. But it was hard to find the right places to put the barrels and find the right people to look after them.

The Criterion Hotel in Oamaru took the first casks — I would deliver them by hand in my Ford Escort van, around eight barrels a week. I had 30 of these barrels. Each barrel was slightly different. I had to calibrate each one and write the measure on the side for customs and excise purposes. Some were 28.5 litres, others 29.5 — it was a pain in the arse.

Not many people were ready to serve beer from wooden barrels, and I wasn't ready for the sheer amount of hard work involved in cleaning them. I used washing soda to clean the barrels — I had to rock them back and forwards, tip them up, rinse them out with water, rock them back and forth, tip them up, rinse them out again . . . it took about 30 minutes to clean a barrel. It was a lot of hard work.

I kept a whiteboard of who had my kegs and I knew roughly how fast they took to finish them. When my chart showed a keg should be ready to pick up I'd race around and get it — I couldn't afford to wait for them to bring it back to me — then I'd clean it, fill it and get it out again. As we grew, it became too hard to monitor the board, but it helped in the early days to make my investment work hard.

The barrels were not without their problems. Many bar staff didn't know how to use them and I had to adapt them to make them more user-friendly compared with traditional English casks.

I remember getting a cask into Rosie O'Grady's, an Irish bar which was just about to open. It was quite frustrating trying to explain to people how handpumps operated. I was trying to find someone to show them how it worked, but it was bedlam and I couldn't get anyone's attention. I had to get back to the brewery, so I left the cask there and I later heard that when the first person came in ordering London Porter, the bar person pulled the handpump and beer shot into the glass, hit the bottom and sprayed everywhere. Finally, they got the hint that they had to learn how to operate them.

The cask was also on top of the bar and it was too hard to lift to put back in the chiller overnight, so the beer got warmer and warmer. I often had to go in and put it back in the chiller myself. I had to take some beer back because it got too warm — I gave them a credit for it and it hurt me financially, but I couldn't afford to have bad-quality beer being sold.

The original board of directors for Emerson's comprised George, Graeme Berry and Alistair Smillie. The three older men oversaw the financial side of business while Richard brewed. Alone.

George continued working in the biochemistry department, but each lunchtime he'd walk the three blocks from the university to the brewery to check on his son. Ingrid would also call by and glue labels on bottles. But for days and months — years even — Richard worked alone, interrupted by the odd customer who wanted to buy something from the cellar door. Not that Richard had time to dwell on his isolation. Detailed handwritten notes show a succession of brews occupied the bulk of each day. Richard recorded when he entered the brewery and when he finished — and it's fair to say very few days clocked in at less than 12 hours.

He put down his first batch of beer on 15 January 1993. The handwritten brew-day notes reveal that the day got off to an inauspicious start when Richard arrived at the brewery to find the water in the hot liquor tank had not heated to the required level overnight. That pushed back the inaugural brew by several hours as he waited for the water to reheat — which came with an additional cost because the electricity usage switched to the day rate from the cheaper night rate. Richard spent 16 hours at 4 Grange Street that day.

That first batch totalled 1068 litres according to the customs and excise form showing duty payable of $896.36. The revenue amounted to about $2.50 a litre. The bulk of the beer went into kegs — around 700 litres — with the rest sold in 500ml plastic bottles retailing for $2.90. The first month's sales totalled $2661.

The bottles came in two shapes — a squat 'grenade' shape and a taller soft-drink-style bottle. Richard regretted the plastic bottles. He knew they presented the wrong image for his sophisticated brand, but he had no choice. Unwilling to put his beer into 750ml bottles, as that would make them look too mainstream (too bogan in his words), he'd also worked out 330ml bottles proved economically unviable for a small brewery thanks to

Bottling by hand was an arduous task but Richard developed strong hands from manually screwing on hundreds of caps.

the tiny margin on each bottle. Besides, he wanted to sell the beer in 500ml bottles — the ideal size for a pint at home. He wanted to use glass but as no other brewers put beer into 500ml glass bottles, no one made them — and no one wanted to make the small number Emerson's needed.

The first media for Emerson's brewery came on 31 January 1993 in the *Dunedin Star Weekender* under the headline '18th-century ale almost ready'. David Stedman believed his father had a hand in giving the story more prominence than it possibly deserved.

As managing editor of *The Star*, Richard Stedman would have known his son's friend had embarked on a new adventure. But just to make sure he knew, George would have called in to remind him. George had been a frequent visitor to the newspaper office when setting up the Otago Excursion Train Trust and he had no qualms doing the same for his son's venture.

The front-page picture shows an innocent-looking Richard — he appears to be a teenager though he's 28 at the time — its caption stating 'Emerson Brewing Co is one of the first of a new breed of small breweries opening around the country'. The full story on page three sits above a piece noting that 10 cruise ships would visit in Dunedin that year. The growth of Emerson's and the rate of increase in cruise ships to the city could be correlated somehow with around 120 ships docking at Port Chalmers in 2018.

In another early interview, Richard said: 'I'm not taking on the big boys. It's a boutique brewery that is promoting and then answering a growing sophistication in people's beer tastes. It's a one-man operation and I want to keep it local. I'm a perfectionist when it comes to the malty flavour of my beer and I want my product to become known for its quality.'

Brewing, bottling and labelling beer can be intensive at the best of times, more so when each process is done by hand. Initially, Richard filled bottles individually — but as 100 to 200 bottles a month in the early days turned into thousands per month, he needed to find another method. With no money to spend on a bottling machine — and besides, his volumes were too small to justify such an expense — he did what he'd always done: he improvised.

I was rummaging around a scrapyard one day when I found the remains of an old three-head vacuum filler and I thought, 'I can make this work.' I reversed the function of the vacuum and I used that filler for the first nine years of the business — doing all the filling by hand.

With that three-head filler, I could do 200 bottles an hour if I was lucky and depending on how many cups of coffee I'd had. I found it incredibly difficult. I was by myself and if someone came to the door to buy beer I had to stop what I was doing, go to the door, sell the beer, have a conversation . . . and by the time I got back to the bottling, I would have to waste beer because it had warmed up and I couldn't keep it consistent. I got sick of the interruptions during the day, so I filled my work day with other tasks, went home in the evening to get something to eat and came back at night to bottle uninterrupted, so I could get a better consistency with filling and carbonation.

The brewery records show gradual, but steady, growth in the first few years. Emerson's couldn't dream of making the list of New Zealand's fastest-growing companies — unlike some craft breweries in recent years. From a grand total of 12,000 litres brewed in the first year, the brewery expanded to around 17,000 litres by the third year. To get an idea of how much things have changed, Emerson's now makes around 12,000 litres of beer a day.

Richard didn't earn a cent for the first year or more. His first pay day in 1994 delivered him the princely sum of $299.00 a fortnight. As an hourly rate — given the fact he slaved away for up to 100 hours a week — it worked out at less than $2 per hour. 'Some weeks I'd do 100 hours — brewing beer in the day, bottling at night, or going to bars to educate people. Educating people took a lot of work because they couldn't comprehend a beer that wasn't a DB Draught or Lion Brown.'

Richard refused to let his deafness stop him, but he found it problematic nonetheless. He'd equipped the brewery with a flashing light rather than a doorbell to alert him to the presence of customers. But he couldn't have a conversation when the phone rang — and in the early days most calls came from people wanting to place orders, so they couldn't go unattended. Instead Richard had to rely on George or the staff at Stewart's Coffee across the road who happily helped out in exchange for a few beers.

Richard's deafness proved more than useful a few years down the track, however. A scam artist chasing the brewery looking for payment for advertising sent a fake invoice. Richard insisted the bill not be paid, but George didn't want to make the mistake of not paying his bills. When a second invoice came, Richard told his father, 'Don't you dare pay this one.'

In chasing their missing 'payment' the fraudster called the brewery asking when the payment would be made, saying it had been authorised

by Richard. The staffer who answered the phone, Tom Jones, asked how Richard had authorised the payment.

'We spoke to him on the phone the other day,' was their response.

Tom replied, 'You know he's deaf, don't you?' The phone went dead and the scam came to an embarrassing halt.

I had an answerphone with a fax in the brewery. If I got a message the light would flash on the answer machine so I'd ring George's number at the biochemistry department and listen intently to see if I could hear him pick up. If he answered I'd just blurt out: 'Dad, there's a message on the answerphone, can you check it out please. Bye.' And I'd hang up.

Dad would ring the answerphone remotely, write down the message and fax it back to me — usually it was a beer order. It took me a while to get customers to send me a fax directly rather than ring.

If I couldn't get hold of Dad, I would walk over to Stewart's Coffee across the road and ask them to check the message — they were happy to do that because I gave them some beer on Friday afternoon.

George Emerson at the opening of the second brewery at 9 Grange Street.

"I WAS ALWAYS GROVELLING FOR A LITTLE BIT MORE MONEY TO MAKE LIFE EASIER. HE'D JUST SAY, 'GET BACK IN THERE AND KEEP MAKING BEER!'"

As a major shareholder, fundraiser, father of the brewer and amateur bookkeeper, George became a de facto chief executive by default in those early days.

Not long after the brewery started, George took early retirement from his job at the university and became a more regular visitor to the brewery where he would keep a frugal eye on the operations.

Helen Emerson understood her father's rationale for the tight economic approach. 'Dad was fiscally conservative to start with and would have thought there was a big enough risk in what he had put in already. No one in the family had run a business before, they were all academics, doctors and teachers. He had done many railway projects, but he had no business experience, so he was risk averse in that sense. And he also felt a responsibility for what he was doing with other people's money — it was a huge responsibility to ask family friends for money for his son.'

I only had one pump for the whole brewery and a wee magnetic pump to move the sparge water from the hot liquor tank into the mash tun. I asked Dad if I could spend just $500 for another pump as it would make my day so much easier and I'd save hours, but he said no.

I was always grovelling for a little bit more money to make life easier. He'd just say, 'Get back in there and keep making beer!'

George was fun to be with at work — we'd talk about trains and have a beer at the end of the day — but I would get so angry at him for not letting us spend money. He was the bookkeeper for the brewery and he was a bloody hard taskmaster — he wouldn't let me spend any money in the first three or four years, which I found extremely frustrating. I would argue with him because I felt if we'd spent a little bit of money it would make life easier. It meant I was overworked and underpaid for a long time.

BARRELS, HANDPUMPS, PORTERS AND PILS

Visiting England in 1990, Richard loved frequenting The Orange, a historic brewpub in London's Pimlico. Inspired by the porter they had on handpull, he asked for the recipe and, on his return to Dunedin, it became the basis for his own London Porter.

Richard checks the clarity on one of his early brews. Photo by Geoff Griggs.

Richard had no qualms starting off with a borrowed recipe — noting that by the time he used the malts available to him in New Zealand, as well as local hops and Dunedin water, a completely different beer presented itself.

Richard Emerson designed his beers to deliver flavour and a unique drinking experience — he wanted to transport the drinker to those British pubs he had so enjoyed in Edinburgh as a teenager and then later on his beer-scouting expedition to Europe. He wanted people to appreciate a complex, tasty beer served at the right temperature and with the low level of carbonation associated with 'real ale' as opposed to the standard-issue, fizzy, highly carbonated beers that were commonplace in New Zealand.

Shrewdly, he realised price and brand would come into the mix. He needed to do more than put a beer to market and trust that people would love it — in fact, he knew some people would hate it.

In the original business plan for Emerson's, Richard detailed the idea that branding could possibly carry more weight than flavour. He noted that people identified themselves with beer brands — as a 'Speight's southern man' or a 'Steinlager-type', and that they chose to project that image through their drinking. 'This is reinforced by the prolific use of beer brands on clothes,' the business plan observed.

He recognised his beers would not be bought 'on rational grounds . . . I believe this is a game played on emotive rules and our objective is to create a certain market who perceive themselves to be "Emerson's drinkers" and in doing so they project a certain self-image.

'The brand image will be created in spite of, or even because of, our higher price. Price does impute quality and a high price can be used to create an image on its own. We are trying to find a niche in a marketplace that is very sophisticated in its brand positioning and we must study the water very carefully before diving in.'

And study it he did. Richard scoured bottle shops and supermarkets to look at pricing — he wanted his beer priced at a premium level well above that of Speight's and other mainstream beer brands. But, equally, he couldn't go so high as to be off-putting — especially as the first beer he was trying to sell was a porter. The only comparable beer on the market was Guinness, so it became a benchmark for pricing, with Emerson's London Porter priced just under the imported Irish brew.

To launch his business with an arcane beer style, served in a fashion many Kiwis despised and openly mocked as 'warm and flat', begged the question — why?

In watching the Emerson's journey over a quarter-century, long-time beer writer and judge Geoff Griggs remains astonished the brand took off on the back of London Porter. As an Englishman, Griggs could well understand the allure of a creamy, chocolatey porter served at the right temperature and with low carbonation, but he couldn't imagine how Richard thought it would resonate with the New Zealand drinking public who had virtually no concept of what they were being served. 'Aside from the fact no one was making craft beer and they certainly weren't calling it craft beer — let alone attempting to sell it in an unopen market — to launch your business with a porter when there were no other dark beers of note, except Guinness, was an incredibly brave — or stupid — thing to do.'

London Porter has incrementally changed over the years, as Richard got access to new malts and different hops — but the fact it's been an award-winning flagship beer for over 25 years and remains relevant today is a testament to how far ahead of its time it was.

Why did you make London Porter your first beer — what were you thinking?
People ask me this a lot. There were several reasons for it.

First, there were not many dark beers on the market. Speight's had just brought out old dark but that didn't have enough flavour. Second, putting a porter in wooden barrels and serving it with a handpump to get a creamy head was unusual, a point of difference.

And third, I couldn't afford a filter to make bright beer, it would have looked hazy. With London Porter being a dark beer you couldn't see that it wasn't a clear beer. Making a dark beer meant I could get away with poor clarity until I got more experienced in the techniques for brighter beer.

All of Emerson's early beers had a classical theme. The second beer off the production line was a German Weissbier. Having fallen out of vogue slightly, the style of beer no longer holds its place at the Emerson's table, but back in the 1990s it stood out, even if it remained misunderstood. On one hand, it was an international award winner, and on the other, it was completely foreign to most punters in New Zealand.

I can recall being at a bar one day to launch my Weissbier and I was so happy to be pouring it with a big foamy head — just right — and I proudly handed it over to the customer who said, 'What the hell is this? Why is there so much foam?'

I told them the foam was an integral part of the beer. He looked at me with suspicion, but eventually took a sip and said, 'Not bad . . .' and walked off. I often felt like I was trying to educate bogans.

Richard had less trouble selling the 1812 Pale Ale. The 1812 has continued to sell well since its inception more than 25 years ago although it's changed its garb from a traditional British-style pale ale to having a more American-influenced spin in keeping with the trends of recent years.

After London Porter I wanted to stick to a Victorian theme and the name 1812 suited that. People also made the association with Beethoven's *1812 Overture*, but the real reason for that name was our phone number at the brewery — 477-1812!

Dad and I thought the name had a good ring to it. Ring to it. Get it? And if anyone mentioned the *1812 Overture*, I said, 'Yes, an overture of hops.'

Richard won a trophy at the Australian International Beer Awards for his Weissbier, but was so poor he needed sponsorship to fly to Melbourne for the awards and had to buy a second-hand suit.

1812

The 1812 Hoppy Pale Ale took its name from the last four digits of the Emerson's Brewery phone number. But Richard also liked the reference to Beethoven's *1812 Overture*, a reference British beer writer Michael Jackson riffed off when describing 1812 as having an 'overture of hops'.

At one stage, Jackson featured 1812 as one of his top 500 beers in the world. The original recipe for 1812 was quite malty and the beer was more a British-style pale ale with hints of caramel and marmalade. It evolved over the years to keep pace with the changing tastes and the changing nature of pale ale, and is now more American-influenced, with a slightly leaner, cleaner malt base. It is the very definition of a session-able pale ale, with loads of flavour and great drinkability.

While London Porter launched Emerson's, the beer that applied the afterburners to the growth of the business came in the form of another highly original, distinctive and enduring creation — a 3.7 per cent English-style bitter, distinguished by the use of New Zealand hops, all created from a recipe scribbled on the back of an envelope.

Richard had created a presence for himself in Oamaru, with the Criterion Hotel being the first pub to take his beer. The city also has a distinctive Victorian charm that seemed to align nicely with the Emerson's brand. There Richard found a friend and devout supporter in Michael O'Brien, now a brewer himself as part of Oamaru's Craftwork Brewery with his partner Lee-Ann Scotti.

Emerson's beers found such success in Oamaru, O'Brien urged Richard to relocate the brewery north of the Waitaki River. For Richard to move from Dunedin didn't bear thinking about. 'I wasn't prepared to completely change my lifestyle to move up there,' he said.

Richard had already committed to pouring two of his beers — London Porter and 1812 — at a Victorian fete in Oamaru, and he thought it would be great to have a third beer on tap.

Richard at the Criterion Hotel in Oamaru.

I wanted to make a four-pinter beer, low in alcohol compared with London Porter and 1812. I wrote the recipe on the back of an envelope the night before I made it. I wanted it juicy and refreshing. I used a touch of black malt to change the pH and the colour. I used some New Zealand hops and it was just what I was looking for. But what do I call it? I knew Michael O'Brien was a bookbinder in Oamaru, and my friend David Stedman was also a bookbinder in Dunedin. That was it: Bookbinder. It went down really well.

Bookie, as the beer became affectionately known, took Wellington by storm in the mid-nineties and helped push Emerson's profile in the beer-centric capital.

If Bookie stole punters' hearts, Emerson's Pilsner changed their minds and turned the brewing industry on its head. That revolutionary brew set Richard Emerson apart and gave him a place in global brewing history.

Created in 1995, Emerson's Pilsner was so far ahead of its time, it took another decade or more for the rest of the industry to catch up. Completely different to anything else in the world at the time, it redefined what New Zealand beer could be — no exaggeration.

A product of a unique set of circumstances, Emerson's Pilsner spurred

To spread the word about Emerson's in the early days, Richard was also pouring beer at events and festivals.

PILSNER

Emerson's Pilsner is a landmark beer in New Zealand history. Just as Steinlager changed the beer landscape when it launched in the 1950s, so Emerson's Pilsner created a ripple effect with the way it showcased New Zealand hops in 1995. Richard set out to create a unique beer, and by taking a classical recipe and replacing herbal, spicy hops with the tropical fruit qualities of New Zealand hops he conjured up a style of beer that has slowly gained acceptance around the world as a definitive Kiwi beer.

Emerson's Pilsner literally changed brewing in New Zealand, brought attention to the quality of Nelson-grown hops and created a flavour profile that was replicated the length and breadth of the country. It's fruity, zesty, crisp and refreshing.

a specific style category now recognised around the world as New Zealand Pilsner. The brewing and beer judging world recognises more than 100 styles, some dating back hundreds of years. New Zealand Pilsner recently joined those ranks and beer competitions around the world have categories dedicated to the unique Kiwi creation.

Richard's contribution to that cannot be understated. He was the first brewer to successfully take a classic European beer and give it an idiosyncratic New Zealand twist with the use of Nelson-grown hops, which were bouncing with tropical fruit characters.

'Emerson's Pilsner is legendary,' says Pete Gillespie, the extraordinarily creative brewer and co-founder at Wellington's Garage Project. 'It's a beer that created a style and you don't get those very often. Sierra Nevada Pale Ale is an example of a beer that created a style and that's what Richard did with Emerson's Pilsner.'

'Emerson's Pilsner turned New Zealand brewing on its head,' adds Kelly Ryan of Fork Brewcorp in Wellington. 'It's so far-reaching in terms of what he's given to the brewing world.'

Richard's quantum leap came when representatives of the organic industry approached him to make an organic beer for them.

I wanted to make a lager completely different to all other lagers and, wow, it had a unique flavour. I told myself at the time that this was the Sauvignon Blanc of beers. I've always wanted to put Dunedin on the beer map. Dunedin water is very similar to the water they use to make Pilsner Urquell in the Czech Republic. People tend to knock Dunedin and I wanted to turn that around and be able to say we've got world-class beer here.

The beer started out as New Zealand BioGrains' Pride of the Plains Pilsner, but it grew so popular Richard decided to put it out under his own label while keeping the original imagery of the Canterbury Plains backed by the Southern Alps. Now known simply as Emerson's Pilsner, it is the company's flagship beer, and a 'gateway' beer for countless craft converts.

What set Emerson's Pilsner apart from anything else being done at the time? Traditional Pilsner — born in the Czech Republic and tweaked in Germany — is best understood via the likes of Heineken, Stella Artois or Carlsberg. It's a snappy lager style with hops that deliver a grassy, herbal or earthy bite. Most people know the flavour profile — it's almost ubiquitous in green-bottled international lagers.

Richard took the classic Pilsner base and overlaid it with New Zealand hops, specifically a hop variety known in those early days as Saaz-D, later to be renamed as what we now refer to as Riwaka. It's not a particularly bitter hop, but it packs strong fruit character including notes of grapefruit and passionfruit.

These days Kiwi brewers have stretched and tweaked New Zealand Pilsner, further accentuating the hops, and many have moved a long way from the jumping-off point created by Emerson's, but all those beers owe their existence to Richard's determination to create something with a wow factor.

Old 95 has also stayed in commission since the early days of the brewery. A barley-wine-style beer made annually and aged to be perfectly smooth and rich for Christmas-time drinking, the first two versions carried the monikers Old 93 and Old 94.

'In the first year I made an Old Ale — designed as a Christmas Ale — and very similar to Old 95, I put them in half-size champagne bottles with a plastic cork. But because an Old Ale is not highly carbonated, people struggled to get the cork out of the bottle. Some people brought them to the brewery and said, "I can't open this." I'd grab the bottle and "pop" — the cork would come out. But that's because I had such strong hands from all the hand-bottling and lifting I'd done!'

While Richard enjoyed the first iterations of that beer, he also struggled to nail the exact flavour he wanted. He soon realised that trying to make an English-style ale with malt designed for New Zealand lagers meant it lacked the depth and character he sought. But in 1995, fellow comic-book enthusiast David Cryer started his malt business, Cryermalt, and began importing specialist malts from Britain and Germany.

What a revelation! Suddenly I got the flavour I wanted. 'That was in 1995 and that's why the Old Ale has been permanently named Old 95.

David Cryer was also a godsend for us. Bringing in the malt we wanted and getting us out of plastic bottles at the same time. David helped me track down a glass-bottle supplier in the UK, so I was able to make a transition from plastic to glass, which was a better image for us.

I was too small-fry for bottle manufacturers in New Zealand to deal with — and I didn't want to go to 330ml bottles as it was just too difficult to make money off them. I didn't want to go to 750ml because they were seen as bogan bottles. And I liked 500ml because that was like having a pint. David brought in the 500ml glass bottles from the UK with containers of malt. It was a little bit more expensive for us, but it was important for our image.

Eventually, we went to a German supplier and now the bottles are done by a New Zealand manufacturer, but we had to change the shape slightly to avoid copyright infringement. This became the mainstay of our packaging and we never considered 330ml bottles until we moved into Anzac Ave — by the time we got there the whole market had changed and now we've even got cans.

It wasn't all success after success for Emerson's though. One beer that failed to stay the course was the briefly famous Dunedin Brown Ale aka DBA.

When I made a beer called DBA, Dunedin Brown Ale, down at the Inch Bar, they nicknamed it the Deaf Bastard Ale. But DB — the brewery, not the deaf bastard — tapped me on the shoulder and said, 'Hey, that's too much like us!' So, I had to stop making that one. It was a nice beer, but it was better to stop brewing it. I never wanted to get offside with anyone — it was all about being diplomatic.

When Richard set off on his beer journey around Europe in 1990, he did so with Michael Jackson's *Pocket Guide to Beer* as his atlas. The journey came full circle when British beer writer Jackson — known as The Beer Hunter — visited New Zealand in 1997 as chief judge at the New Zealand Beer Awards. Emerson's won the top prizes for 1812, Weissbeer and Dunkelweizen, a dark wheat beer. They also earned a lifelong fan in Jackson.

Born in the English city of Leeds, BBC journalist Michael Jackson fell in love with beer, particularly the beer and the beer-making traditions of Belgium. He launched his beer-writing with his 1977 book *The World Guide to Beer*, in which he tried to define the different styles of beer around the world. He also wrote at length about the aroma and taste of beer. His popularity in America became entrenched with *The Beer Hunter*, a six-part documentary series made in 1990, which was widely credited as the catalyst for the American microbrewery explosion of the mid-1990s.

Given all the beers he'd tasted around the world in his decades of beer appreciation, any praise from Jackson comes gold-plated. After visiting New Zealand, Jackson wrote glowingly on his website about Emerson's:

A beer lover named Jim Sepiol, who was blind, guided me round Boston on my first visit there many years ago, jumping on and off the subway with a dexterity that alarmed me. 'Watch where you are going!' he admonished. To mock one's own misfortunes suggests a very robust spirit.

Jim worked as a consultant appraising flavours and fragrances. I asked

Famed beer writer Michael Jackson visited New Zealand in 1997 and fell in love with Emerson's beer.

Bottom photo by Geoff Griggs.

him whether he thought that the serious impairment of his eyesight heightened his other senses. He said he did not know — I suspect he had heard that question more often than he cared. Jim died a while back, but he will never depart my memory.

It sounds *Reader's Digest*-ish to say that such encounters are humbling, but there is no escaping that feeling. In the Pacific Northwest, I once encountered a homebrew club for the hearing-impaired. It was called The Grateful Deaf.

Having had the most minor problems with my own hearing, I cannot imagine how anyone copes with deafness. Brewer Richard Emerson was born almost completely deaf because his mother had rubella. 'When I meet a nice girl, I tell her I have Aids,' he jokes, blackly. 'But I explain that I take them out when I go to bed.'

Friends mention that Richard has a very good nose, and is (as I heard for myself) very fluent in descriptors. He, too, is probably tired of being asked about that.

No one wants to be defined by a handicap — or, for that matter, some supposed advantage. Richard Emerson is a brewer in his native New Zealand. He makes the best range of beers that I tasted on a recent tour in his country.

I met Richard at the New Zealand Brewersfest, where he won no fewer than four medals. There was a silver for his fruity, winey, Bookbinder Bitter, and an astonishing three golds, for: 1812 IPA, very English-tasting, refreshing and spicily hoppy, with beautifully combined flavours; a Weissbier (made with a Weihenstephan yeast), offering notes of sherbet, banana, apple and clove; and a Dunkelweizen, soft, spicy and full of ripe banana flavors. Not surprisingly, he emerged as supreme champion.

I was asked to hand out the awards, and I invited each winner to say a few words. When it came to Richard, I shamefully hesitated. His deafness also affects his speech; would he wish to address an audience? Magically, the mike found its way into his hands, and he eloquently expressed his delight.

That Michael Jackson book meant a lot to me and later in life I got to meet him. He loved our Weissbier. He thought Bookbinder was a great example of a session beer. I'm proud to be recorded in Michael Jackson's beer books. But when he came here, the New Zealand public wasn't ready for him. It was great for him to raise awareness among craft brewers — I'm glad he came here — I think a lot of things changed within the brewing industry after he came here.

CHAPTER

9

MARRIED TO A BREWERY

I was naïve and didn't have much chance to have relationships with women because of my lack of communication. I couldn't ask for a phone number, it was a bloody nuisance. I couldn't ring up a girl — if I did, I would have had to get someone to do it for me. It was difficult unless I could talk to them face to face — I really had no privacy and that made it quite hard, so, really I never had any luck with dates.

Richard's first wife Marian Rait labels a bottle of London Porter. In the early years of the brewery family members did all the manual labour – from labelling to bottling to delivering beer.

I did manage a date or two when I was in London because I was with people on a daily basis in the operating theatre. Apart from that it was rare to have a relationship. When I came back from the UK in 1990, my sister Helen had a friend, Marian, and she gave me the signals she was interested in me which was a surprise — I wasn't used to women being interested in me.

We started going out. She was quite shy, but she was happy to help me in the brewery in the early days. We used the company van to go on our honeymoon — we put a mattress in the back and went up the West Coast. As life went on, things changed — we had different views on life.

Richard Emerson is not the first brewer to see the demands of the business take its toll on relationships. The long hours, the low pay, the unrelenting demands of feeding a constantly hungry beast conspire to deliver an unbearable amount of stress.

Equally, Richard's fledgling business may not have survived those early years without the input and support of his first wife, Marian Rait.

The marriage ended unhappily, for all the reasons many marriages break down — loss of trust, miscommunication, financial stress, work stress — but it also started the way most relationships do: happily.

Marian, who was studying to be a teacher, had taken music papers at Otago University where she met Helen Emerson. At the time, Richard was overseas on his beer-discovery journey. When he returned home, Richard moved back into his parents' house where Marian visited — to see Helen.

Before long, Richard became the reason to visit. With Helen's connection to Marian, a solution to Richard's usual inability to call to arrange a date presented itself — he could trust Helen with his privacy and she played the go-between role, ringing her friend to arrange dates with her brother.

'In those days, Richard was young and fun and full of enthusiasm,' Marian said. 'He'd just come back from overseas and had the taste of the beer in Europe. He was highly driven and had this really cool idea to start a brewery.'

Marian remembered a 'socially awkward' young man who could be a bit immature. 'But that was to do with his deafness and not being able to read social situations that well. He was also self-conscious of his hearing aids in those days — he wanted to cut his hair but was worried about his hearing aids showing. And I said go for it.'

As time went on, she also discovered Richard's energy and passion for his brewery could make him too focused on himself and often unaware of what other people did to help him. 'Being so enthusiastic, he often came across as overly self-focused and he did forget important things to do with other people, such as birthdays.'

Richard and Marian had a long and often happy relationship. They lived together for a while in a flat Richard shared with his old friend Grant Hanan — a period when Marian witnessed first-hand the success of the pilot plant in Ravensbourne. 'I remember going around on the back of the motorbike to the garage in Ravensbourne and writing the numbers on the bottle caps for which brew it was. Then they'd go out to his friends for feedback and London Porter was always a good one.'

Friends from that time remembered a couple who worked well together, though there was some scepticism when Richard announced they would be getting married in January 1995.

Marian was Richard's first serious girlfriend and some of his friends believed he rushed into the marriage, with one believing Richard had struggled to build relationships because of his disability and therefore jumped at the first chance he got. 'Richard always had an eye for the

Marian witnessed first-hand how tough it was for Richard in the early years.

girls and was fascinated by them, but it was hard for him — and he was a handsome guy, but he didn't have much luck with women.'

Others worried about Richard and Marian's quite distinctive personalities. Richard loved being with outgoing, expressive and upbeat people with whom he could easily communicate and who brought fun and laughs, while Marian tended to be shy and introverted.

On the flip side, others worried Richard's riveted devotion to the brewery made him a difficult person to be around.

According to Rob Smillie, 'Richard can get so focused on what he's doing, he can forget other people in his life. The early years of marriage would have been hard on Marian — he was so busy with the business and she felt isolated. When they eventually split up I thought it was good for both of them because they were both unhappy in that marriage.'

David Stedman agreed. 'Marian was a complicated person. They would often have arguments that would leave Richard distraught and in tears. But Richard can also be very focused — single-minded and tunnel-visioned — and sometimes he doesn't think about the consequences to his nearest and dearest. He survived that marriage by denial. After my own marriage ended, he was determined, saying, "That's not going to happen to me."'

Marian saw more than anyone — more than George and Ingrid — how much of a toll the first five years of the business took and how much love and support Richard required from his family in order to survive.

Richard had set himself a goal of making it past the first five years in business because he'd been told that 95 per cent of start-up businesses didn't make it that far. Whether that's true or merely a truism designed to motivate young businesses to keep ploughing on is neither here nor there, as for Richard — and for George — those first five years became a mountain they needed to climb in order to see how far they might go.

'It was stressful, fun and exciting,' Marian recalled, noting the feeling of camaraderie as she and Ingrid would work next to each other bottling beer on the three-head filling machine Richard had salvaged from the scrapyard, or hand-gluing labels onto plastic bottles. It took painstaking precision to paint on the glue with a tacky brush — 'Oh, the joy of a new brush that wasn't all tacky!' — and then roll the label onto the bottle straight and in the right position.

Deliveries to make, festivals to attend, orders to process over the phone — the workflow was incessant. 'I'd make business calls on his behalf because the landline wasn't an option for him. There was lots of lifting — bottles, boxes, barrels — it was very labour intensive for us all; Richard, George, Ingrid, Helen and me.

'I remember at Christmas delivering wooden barrels of beer to a backpackers in town — it was full of international travellers and to make them feel more at home we'd take a barrel and handpump around on Christmas Day and then head off to our own Christmas dinner.

'And then there were beer festivals — jumping into a car on a Friday night after a full week of work and heading away to pour beer at things like Blues, Brews and BBQs.'

FOR RICHARD — AND FOR GEORGE — THOSE FIRST FIVE YEARS BECAME A MOUNTAIN THEY NEEDED TO CLIMB IN ORDER TO SEE HOW FAR THEY MIGHT GO.

One of the more fascinating tasks for Marian came on a trip to the United States where the couple visited 22 breweries in two weeks as Richard researched bottling machines. The trip culminated in a visit to a bottling-line manufacturer for a full day's tutorial. Richard struggled with this kind of learning experience — where someone might be pointing to a piece of equipment and talking in the direction of the object rather than to him. 'So, there I was taking notes on this bottling machine because Richard doesn't pick up everything. I was his back-up — I learned a lot about bottling machines!'

While the family support for Richard delivered critical sustenance for the early survival of the brewery, it also came with huge amounts of tension. Watching the father–son relationship at a distance, Marian could see why George tried to keep a tight rein on the finances in order to build something for Richard's future.

George had always feared for Richard, worried that his son's disability would hinder his career, worried that he might not find the work required to see him through to retirement. He knew the brewery might be the one opportunity Richard had been waiting for in life. But to make that happen, he needed to take a financial risk — with his own money and the money of his friends and family.

'The business was always a risk — and even to get it started, Richard had to convince George to bankroll it. But George didn't have business in his background — he was from academia — he didn't know how to set up a business or how to run a business.

'He came from a frugal background to start with and it was a huge step for him to undertake the setting up of a business. He felt personally responsible for getting his friends into this situation with their money; banking on his son's success. But as a son, Richard thought his dad was grumpy and conservative for keeping a tight rein on the money.

'George and Richard did have differences of opinion and both of them had a fault of not listening to other people — I might have an idea or Ingrid would have an idea and they'd say, "No, no, no," but two weeks later it was "Tick, tick, tick . . ." and they'd have the same idea.'

From a detached position, Marian believed the oversight provided by that first board of directors — George, Graeme Berry and Alastair Smillie — ensured the brewery made it through the teething years. 'Those three guys were amazing and only ever wanted the best for the brewery. They wanted the business to make it past those first five years.'

The other thing that astonished and troubled Marian was Richard's work ethic. Always a driven person, the physical energy and ultimate responsibility for making the brewery work fell squarely on his shoulders and sometimes the weight became too much to bear.

'I can remember times when he'd come home in tears and say, "I'm giving it up." And I'd be talking him through, saying keep going, keep going.

'The first brew day alone was sixteen hours and after that it was relentless — continuous eleven- and twelve-hour days. And not just the physical aspect, it was all the decisions, the work that had to be done, the mistakes that might happen, the problems that needed to be solved — things would just stack up and suddenly he's in tears saying, "I can't do it any longer, I want to give it up" — it was heartbreaking to see and I don't think he would have been like that in front of his mum and dad. But at six o'clock the next morning, he was back to work. His work ethic was extraordinary.'

This is where a crack started to appear in the relationship — Richard's commitment to a business where demands pounded like an incessant drum and finances were tight as a guitar string, raised his own tension and that, in turn, made him more focused on proving himself. Marian did her best to support him — by working in the brewery, providing the hot meal he needed at the end of the day, pursuing her own career, helping provide financial stability — and she felt Richard didn't appreciate that nor reciprocate it.

'It started off great — of course it did — but both of us had full-time jobs. I had my career to think about as well, which was often forgotten. Despite the long hours and the stress, the brewery remained the number one priority for Richard. There was a lot of cool things about the business, but what I didn't like was that it came first, over and above all else — it was brewery first and foremost and then his family, then me.'

Marian also started to resent the drinking culture associated with owning a brewery. 'Let's just say the brewer was never the sober driver. There also became a lot of hangers-on who came around for the free beer — Friday nights turned into a thing where a lot of the people there were not genuine. They were just there for free beer and took advantage — it was getting out of hand.'

Tastings, events, festivals, award dinners . . . their social life inevitably became overtaken by all things beer. In short, the business and the wider industry got in the way of the relationship — they were not what you'd call a normal married couple in that regard.

In 2006, Richard and Marian discussed and agreed on a vital move for Marian to further her career. She enrolled in a year-long postgraduate teaching course at the University of Canterbury. In Christchurch, she boarded with her mother and she travelled back to Dunedin as many weekends and school break times as she could. While they lived apart, the marriage was still intact. However, looking back, Richard felt this time apart marked the beginning of the end of the relationship. They were officially divorced in 2009.

One of the things we did every week was have some drinks and a barbecue on Friday night. They were my advertising budget. That was how we did the marketing by word of mouth, and that was how we built up the brand credibility in Dunedin. It took a long time. People still have memories of the Friday-night sessions — in some ways it helped the brand, but it was also my way of letting off some steam and making people happy. It started off small but it did get out of control.

Ah, the Friday-night parties. Chris O'Leary, who would later move to Dunedin and join the Emerson's team, once came down from Hawke's Bay to visit Richard and arrived as one of the Friday-night sessions ramped up. 'There was a brazier going, music playing, three handpumps set up and people helping themselves to beer. There were about thirty or forty people, and I said to Richard, "This is great, but you didn't have to do this for me!" And he replied, "It's not for you — this happens every Friday."'

Richard loved the Friday nights — an end-of-week wind-down where he could share his passion with a new set of 'appreciators'. He treated the lost revenue as the marketing budget he didn't have. He believed that the more people loved the Emerson's experience, the more they'd talk about it.

And the sessions became a way of saying thank you. It was a few beers for those who helped get him through another week, including the staff at Stewart's Coffee across the road, who would do everything from answering phones to letting Richard use their forklift. Special gratitude extended to Mike Hormann. When he set up his business, Set Point Electronics, at 11 Grange Street, he took great pleasure in seeing his long-lost primary school friend, Richard Emerson, across the road. When Richard had gone to Logan Park, Mike had joined Rob Smillie at Otago Boys' and he and Richard had lost touch, only to be reunited on Grange Street where Hormann happily answered telephone calls and did some electrical work for Richard; he later stored malt in a small shed on his premises when Richard ran out of room across the road. 'I didn't mind doing those things, he owned a brewery after all.'

Hormann even got a great present for some of his clients when Richard got distracted one day and put the wrong amount of malt into a batch of IPA. 'He got a phone call in the middle of it, which meant he had to go away and get someone,' Mike recalled. 'He lost track of how much malt he was putting in and added too much. I said, "What will be wrong with it?" "Well, it won't taste like the beer it's supposed to be?" "Make it anyway," I said, "I'll buy it off you at cost." I got some labels printed with Set Point IPA on them and we bought the lot to give away to our clients!'

When Hormann sold his business to German electronics giant Siemens, George noted his obvious business acumen and invited him to join the Emerson's board of directors. In taking his seat on the other side of the business, he — along with the other directors — realised the Friday-night sessions had amplified to the extent that they'd taken a small toll on the business. 'It was a way of saying thanks to people and it started as one beer and then home. But some of the guys weren't having one. After a while, too many people were drinking too much and at no profit to the company. A lot of the stuff we drank was what they called sweepings — low-filled bottles, end-of-run beer, that sort of thing. But the fact was Emerson's weren't making enough beer — we were selling everything we made — so there wasn't much to give away. I did get a little over those Friday nights because they did get a little bit out of hand — people just turned up to drink beer that had no connection to Emerson's. And when no one's paying for the beer, the directors start doing sums.'

Hormann also played a key role in Emerson's first move — across the road to 9 Grange Street, the premises next door to Set Point Electronics. Mike knew the landlord and negotiated the lease for Richard.

The landmark move showed that not only had Emerson's survived the critical first five years, they'd actually got a seven-year itch of sorts with the original brewery pushed to capacity and ready to burst.

'The brewery was growing at 24 to 25 per cent a year and you just had to keep chucking more stainless steel at it and trying to find more space,' Hormann said.

Richard's transition from one side of Grange Street to the other started in 1999. It marked a massive turning point for the brewery, but a more severe crisis in Richard's life waited up the road.

I would brew at 4 Grange Street and go over to 9 Grange Street at night to paint. I was trying to do everything to save money. Also, my father wasn't terribly well at the time — he started to stumble and lose his balance, I remember him stumbling across the road — so he had less and less involvement at 9 Grange Street and I was doing more work on the accounts. Then we found Dad had cancer and that was a devastation. That was one of the toughest periods of my life.

George would say, 'Don't worry about me, keep working, keep brewing.' He had a brain tumour the size of a ping-pong ball, but he kept pushing me to keep going. He had an operation, but then the cancer came back. But for me it was hard — I had to keep the business going, but when my father ended up in the hospice, I had mixed feelings — I regret not being able to spend more time with him, but I was a victim of circumstance. I had to keep the business going. To watch my father deteriorate wasn't very nice.

10

THE PASSING OF TAIERI GEORGE

With Emerson's brewery evolving into a new stage —
moving to bigger premises, winning awards, gleaning
national attention — George Emerson decided to take
early retirement from the university's biochemistry
department in 1999.

He wanted to spend more time at the brewery with his son, taking a stronger hand in guiding the business to further growth and success. Besides which, as Ingrid observed, he'd seen the writing on the wall at the university. The emphasis on research rather than lecturing didn't suit George, who loved to teach. Not quite at retirement age, he threw in his lot when the university looked to cull staff by offering early retirement.

But just as George decided to take his life in a new direction, his health wavered. He lost his balance and complained of headaches. When Richard first contacted Helen, who was living in London, with the news George was unwell, she took it at face value. 'I got this funny email from Richard saying, "Dad's got a bump on his head."'

SELF-PITY WAS NOT PERMITTED, WALLOWING WAS NOT PERMITTED IN OUR HOUSE — STOICISM WAS THE ORDER OF THE DAY; YOU BUCKLED DOWN AND GOT ON WITH IT. YOU DIDN'T SHOW EMOTION OR CRY.

While she wondered why Richard had emailed her in the middle of the night in New Zealand about a seemingly innocuous accident — she assumed her father had lost his balance, fallen and hit his head — she didn't place any urgency on the information. That evening, she phoned home to speak to her mother, only then discovering her father had not bumped his head but had collapsed. An ambulance rushed him to hospital and he'd undergone an operation on a cancerous brain tumour. 'When I asked Richard later on why he'd been so vague, he said he didn't want to alarm me until he knew what was going on.'

The surgeon removed George's 'ping-pong ball' of tumour, but couldn't get all of the cancer. He gave George 18 months to live. Helen returned home to Dunedin every six months or so, and on these visits she saw a new side to her father. 'The doctors gave him a year to 18 months and, because he was

George Emerson, he was bloody well getting the full 18 months' worth.

'There was anger and frustration for Dad — he was not long retired and he was asking: "Why me? Why now?" It was a side I'd never seen before — the anger and the frustration — but he refused to let anyone else have pity or sympathy for him. He didn't want anyone to wallow. Self-pity was not permitted, wallowing was not permitted in our house — stoicism was the order of the day; you buckled down and got on with it. You didn't show emotion or cry.

'Throughout our lives, Dad had not been demonstrative or affectionate, but he was actually quite an emotional person — it's just that we never properly saw that until he was ill. Richard is also emotional, a heart-on-the-sleeve person. In that regard, Dad and Richard were peas in a pod — so similar — which is why they clashed. Richard seemed to suffer the most as George deteriorated. Ingrid remained her pragmatic self in response to Dad's illness.'

On one of Helen's trips home to Dunedin, the family went together to Central Otago — they checked out a lot of the spots George held dear, places where he used to photograph trains on what had since become the Otago Central Rail Trail. He loved Tiger Hill near Omakau, and the emotion was as stark as the landscape as George stood there for the last time.

'Dad got incredibly sentimental and emotional, and wanted to visit old haunts because he would never see them again — it was very dramatic — and Richard would respond with sentiment and drama, and Mum and I would try to balance it out with pragmatism.

'We took a trip into Central and went over Ophir Bridge — one of those iconic, Central Otago postcard bridges — and then we went to Tiger Hill. Dad broke down and started crying. He said, "I'm never going to see this again," and that just set Richard off. Richard broke down and started crying. We all started crying.'

In that moment, the family realised the enormity of the situation. Ingrid, Richard and Helen knew their patriarch, husband, father, friend would soon be gone . . . and George knew he had to leave behind everything he loved. That moment brought together everything important in George's life: his family, trains, Central Otago, everything he'd done for the Otago Excursion Train Trust, the Taieri Gorge, Richard's brewery — and the knowledge all would outlast him. Like the steam trains he loved, George Emerson's time had come.

Tiger Hill was one of George's favourite spots. It was a formidable grade on the
Otago Central Railway for trains travelling from Alexandra towards Omakau.
It is one of the steepest climbs on the line with added twists that increased the
difficulty of the one in 50 climb. The engine drivers were faced with the task of
nurturing their locomotive with a good head of steam as they roared past the
Chatto Creek pub, crossing State Highway 85 for a mile of straight running then
hitting the one in 50 grade into the first right-hand leg of the S-shaped climb
across the hill. The locomotives would slow down with massive huffs and puffs, the
smoke stacks barking.

The train would cross State Highway 85 a second time then swing into
another hard left-hand curve before disappearing out of sight from the road. As
you drive up the road from Chatto Creek, you would see the train again on the
right. The engine would struggle, wheels slipping on the greasy rails as it made its
way over the final ascent to the peak of the hill where State Highway 85 crosses
the railway for the third time on an overbridge and then the locomotive could
relax as the train coasted down the grade to Omakau.

Dad loved watching those steam trains from strategic spots on Tiger Hill,
where you could see their progress for miles, as far as the Chatto Creek pub.
The smoke from the steam locomotive would signal the presence of the train

George Emerson, seen here on Tiger Hill, loved photographing trains in Central Otago.

approaching. He would check the light conditions with his exposure meter to prepare his camera with the correct shutter-speed and aperture combinations as the steam engine puffed up the hill.

It was fun watching the drama of the train puffing across the landscape. The formidable grade was not the only feature Dad was fascinated with, it was the beauty of the landscape with the railway cutting a large S shape into the side of the hill, the beautiful, massive Dunstan mountain range in the background.

Depending on the time of the day, the lighting conditions would transform rolling Tiger Hill into a surreal scene not too dissimilar to a Rita Angus painting. The gullies blacked out, sunshine on the ridges, shadow-play at its best. George would frequently travel back to Tiger Hill to try to capture the 'perfect shot'. I have plenty of photographs in the collection to attest to that!

Bill Cowan's book *Rails to Cromwell* has a tribute chapter to my father that explains his photography. 'The late George Emerson had a theory about railway photography. He contended that the average railway photographer never strayed more than a few metres from his car to take a photo. George believed that this self-imposed restraint, a laziness perhaps, call it what you will, severely limited the range of photo opportunities available. He was never bound by this restriction; he got out and about.' That quote pretty much sums it up, we had so much fun photographing the trains together before the line was closed in 1990.

George and I would travel in the well-worn Triumph 2000 over the farm track to get into the ridges of the Poolburn Gorge then hike over the farm country until we got the wonderful vista view of the railway on the other side of the gorge. Then it was a game of patience, waiting for the train to arrive. Our worst-case scenario was that the train had already gone through the gorge and we'd be waiting in vain, but this never happened as George always allowed enough time to be ahead of the train. We'd be there, waiting . . . waiting, listening for a faint rumble of the diesel climbing up the grade.

First there was that sound! Then a headlight . . . we'd jump up, check the camera exposure and regain our composure ready to take that perfect photo. Click, click and then we'd watch the train snaking around the curves in the gorge before disappearing into the tunnel. That was our photo for the day, as to try and catch up with the train would be futile as we would have to run across the country, jump into the car, drive over the rough road. There was no point.

The memories of the great times we had there are still emotional for me. Dad loved spring in Central Otago, the blossoms, the green landscape, the shadow-play on the hills, a whisper of snow on the ranges — it's magical country.

In March 2002, just as he turned 67, George deteriorated further and was placed into hospice care. He remained stoic — urging Richard to keep working at the brewery, to not let up because of his illness. When he spoke to Helen in London on her thirtieth birthday, he told her not to rush home for his sake: 'He said, "In your circumstances I wouldn't be coming back to New Zealand to see your dying father either." I could hear Mum across the room saying, "It's just the drugs talking."

'But that was Dad. He'd been in similar circumstances when we were in Edinburgh in 1983. At the time both his parents were quite ill, but he stayed the full duration of his sabbatical. His mother died within days of him getting home and his father just weeks later. We were told his mother had hung on for him to get home. As soon as he got back to New Zealand she went downhill and died very quickly, but he didn't cut short his trip for her.

'Dad's attitude to Richard and the brewery was "Get on with it". Dad's view was that you're not going to throw this away because of me. Richard would have seen the sense of it but nevertheless found it difficult.'

Richard also contacted Helen around the time of her birthday and told her, 'Dad hasn't got long, you should come home.' He also talked his father's doctor into ramping up George's medication to keep him alive and coherent until Helen could get home.

'I flew out at short notice,' Helen said. 'And he was so jacked up on steroids, we had three pretty good weeks in the hospice. We were all there every day. Towards the end, George realised it was borrowed time and asked the doctors to reduce his medication. At one point he said, "This can't go on forever, Helen has to go back to London." And he asked the doctor to stop the steroids.

'While he was working hard, Richard would also be there every day. One night, Richard arranged for a slideshow on the wall of the hospice room — slideshows were part of our family life growing up, it's what you did when you didn't have a TV! And I remember Richard and I feeding Dad teaspoons of beer and whisky.'

Barely conscious, George didn't react when Richard came into his father's room and asked to borrow George's camera gear. He'd decided to take a trainspotting trip up the coast with George's camera as a way to honour him. George couldn't respond, but Ingrid told Richard to go, to take the camera, it belonged to him now.

'It was absolutely the right thing to do, but it meant he wasn't there

'DAD'S ATTITUDE TO RICHARD AND THE BREWERY WAS "GET ON WITH IT". DAD'S VIEW WAS THAT YOU'RE NOT GOING TO THROW THIS AWAY BECAUSE OF ME. RICHARD WOULD HAVE SEEN THE SENSE OF IT BUT NEVERTHELESS FOUND IT DIFFICULT.'

when Dad died,' Helen said. 'Mum and I both thought it was appropriate he was out doing what Dad would have wanted to do on a gorgeous autumn day — using Dad's equipment to photograph trains.'

In fact, no one from the Emerson family was in the room when George passed away. A cleaner had come in, so Ingrid went into the small kitchen to make a cup of tea and Helen stepped through the sliding doors into the garden. 'Suddenly I realised I couldn't hear him breathing — he had this rattling breath at the end. He was gone.'

George Emerson died on 24 March 2002.

Ingrid, Helen and Marian all tried to contact Richard. He had a mobile phone, but had either turned it off or the battery had died. 'There was no way of contacting him,' Helen said. 'We just waited for him to come back.'

Richard returned to a room with the curtains drawn and the doors locked and the news that while he'd been away, his father had died.

I had been visiting George on a daily basis, finishing work and driving up to the hospice. The experience was quite stressful. George always kept telling me, 'Don't lose focus on the brewery. Keep it going.'

On one hand, I had to keep work going and, on the other hand, I wanted to take time off to be with Dad. It was all very frustrating and it didn't take much for me to snap when someone asked me a silly question. George was then struggling, he had faded in and out. At one stage, we thought we had lost him. In fact, he had kind of slipped into a self-induced coma and came out of it after a day or two.

Top: At the hour George Emerson passed away Richard was living out his father's passion — he was in Oamaru taking photographs of trains with George's camera.

Bottom: Richard and Helen share a beer.

That particular day, I knew the mainline steam locomotive Ab663 was going to be steaming back north to the Christchurch depot having completed several excursions while temporarily based in Dunedin. So, I decided to take the opportunity to take a break, grab George's camera and chase the steam engine up the coast as far as Oamaru.

Unbelievably, the weather was good and the Ab-class steam locomotive was only towing a tank wagon with its supply of waste oil. I felt like I had my own steam train for the day as there were no other rail fans around chasing the locomotive — it was awesome. Because it was such a small train itself, I had to think how I wanted to take the photo, pretty much what George would have been thinking.

All this thinking helped to cast aside all my problems, the brewery, Dad's illness and my emotions for the day. It was fantastic to be dashing ahead of the engine looking for the next photo stop, jumping out, preparing the camera and composition . . . click, click and then running back to the car.

At Oamaru, I took the last photograph of the day: the steam engine with the Oamaru town clock in the background, it was a surreal moment as the time shown on the clock is immortalised in my image. It was only when I got back to the hospice later in the day that I realised Dad had passed away at almost that same moment. It was a bittersweet moment. I was glad Dad's camera was being used as a kind of finale, doing what he loved — photographing steam trains.

The beers Richard and Helen had fed to George at the hospice included a trial batch Richard had worked on for years, trying to perfect it, but always coming up short. In that way, it resembled George's attempts to frame the perfect photo at Tiger Hill. Richard knew he had a good beer, but he needed everything to be right — from the flavour, to the name, to the label.

But the beer refused to come fully into focus. It started life as Winter Warmer — a lightly spiced dark ale for the cooler months. It then evolved into 40 Winks — a name that honoured George to a degree because he tended to nod off in his chair after a few drinks.

We used the image of character Ted Bovis from *Hi-de-Hi!* in a bowler hat and holding the beer on his belly. It was the only time I broke away from the established Emerson's format — the label was bright yellow and cartoonish. People didn't like it. They didn't want an arty-farty label, they wanted a good conservative label. New Zealand craft brewing wasn't ready for it, compared with now when you look at a supermarket shelf and it's full of bright, colourful, loud cans.

TAIERI GEORGE

Taieri George is a spiced ale released every year on George Emerson's birthday – 6 March. With spices such as cinnamon and nutmeg, and added honey, the beer is also perfect for Easter. Richard struggled with a name for the beer as he developed it. At one stage is was called Winter Warmer and then 40 Winks. When George passed away, Richard wanted the beer to honour his father, and the inspiration came from an unlikely source when Tom Jones, an Emerson's staff member noticed a certificate on the wall of the Emerson residence. It was given to George by the Dunedin City Council for work he'd done on the Taieri Gorge Railway. Except it featured a typo that said: 'Thank you George Emerson for your work on the Taieri George Railway.' And so Taieri George came to life, a beer dedicated to George Emerson and the trains he loved so much.

As the name and label went through various iterations, Richard battled with the balance between sweet malt, spice and alcohol. Richard had lifted the alcohol to a heady 6.8 per cent, upped the spice levels of cinnamon and nutmeg, and added honey.

One night at the hospice, Richard gave his father a sip of the latest version through a straw. George, unable to speak, simply raised his hand and gave it the thumbs up. Spot on. The chief taster for Emerson's Brewery had given it his seal of approval.

When George passed, Richard wanted the new winter ale to honour his father in some way, and his inspiration came from an unlikely source.

At the reception following George's funeral, 'Tom, one of our staff members, was reading a framed certificate on the wall given to Dad by the Dunedin City Council for work he'd done on the Taieri Gorge Railway. Tom said he'd spotted a typo and he read aloud: "Thank you George Emerson for your work on the Taieri George Railway." '

And so Taieri George came to life, a beer dedicated to George Emerson. A beer dedicated to trains and the railway that George Emerson so loved, and brewed by his son in the brewery George had helped create. The label carries a picture of a train and its annual release date: 6 March — George's birthday. 'I made it Dad's birthday rather than the day of his death as I wanted it to mark his life.'

A NEW
MENTOR AND
A BIGGER
BREWERY

'Richard's dad was everything to him for many years.
George was a strong character in his life and he was really
emotional when George passed away. That was the loss of
a major foundation for him as a person and in business.
George was obstinate and tough, but if it wasn't for his
firmness, Richard wouldn't be where he is now.

Richard has been a great ambassador for New Zealand hops, trialling different varietals as they were developed.

I think he felt it was his role to get Richard to perform or stay on target — "Come on, where's the beer? Get it brewed!" He had such a large influence on Richard's life. He was gruff, funny, intelligent and he was very firm,' said Richard's friend and future colleague Chris O'Leary.

'George directed everything — including Richard — so when George died, Richard had this massive hole. His life coach was gone, his best friend was gone, the person he was afraid of was gone, the person he was proving himself to was gone.'

When George died, the board of directors — led by Graeme Berry — stepped up and took over managing the brewery. George's role of de facto CEO fell to Graeme, who continued to run the business as his friend had done for the preceding decade.

Richard's wife at the time, Marian, noted the undercurrents in the family and business changed at that time. 'Richard did change after George died — the dynamics were different. He respected his father, and the relationship with Graeme Berry, who had stepped into George's role as managing director, wasn't the same — it was more stressful and things were out of balance in his life at that stage. He didn't go off the rails as such, but the dynamics in his friendships changed. It was a difficult time after George passed away. Something wasn't gelling. He might have done things differently if George had still been around.'

Richard continued to run the brewery operation — managing the small but growing number of staff — while Berry looked after the financial side and kept Richard's enthusiasm in check. A meticulous bookkeeper, Berry kept the business on the same steady course George had set up, with growth continuing at around 25 per cent per annum. But he couldn't fulfil the other roles George had provided — father, friend, mentor, go-between.

Dealings between Graeme and Richard nevertheless took on some of the characteristics of the George–Richard relationship, but the battles over money created tension mainly because of Richard's difficulty in 'reading' Graeme.

'As I've said, some people have what I call a radio face. There's little expression. I find those people very hard to read with their straight faces. Graeme Berry has a very deadpan face and I could never quite work him out.'

On bigger-ticket items, instead of dealing with his father, where the underlying current of love and life history provided some cushioning, Richard now had to convince the board when he wanted to do something substantial.

'He didn't like having to present things to the board for approval,' O'Leary said. 'If he wanted new tanks he'd say, "I want them now, I need them." He was probably correct, but he didn't like being questioned over the sums. Graeme was a lot like George, old-school, blunt, but also very hard for Richard to read — and Graeme would get Richard cranked up. With no disrespect to Richard, no one can manage him — there's no way. You have to work off his passions and interests to get him to go in a certain direction. He doesn't like the word no and he doesn't like conflict.'

Richard's creativity sparked a raft of new ideas — new recipes — but the brewery had no capacity to make them. To introduce a new beer would cut down production time for the core range, and then the new beer needed marketing and distribution, which the directors deemed fiscally irresponsible given how tight the operation ran.

Board member Mike Hormann found himself siding with Berry. 'If you're making a whole lot of little beers that might not sell that well, you're doing that at the expense of the core range. At that stage, anything that cut into Pilsner was costing money because that was the best seller. As a board we had to keep saying, "Sorry, Richard." He would come in and say, "I've got this new beer I want to make," and we'd say, "Sorry, Richard. We don't have capacity for it."'

As a compromise, they introduced the Brewer's Reserve range — occasional releases where Richard could express his artistic side.

Richard and the directors also argued over putting up the price of the beer. Emerson's popularity meant Richard's original pricing — pitched in the sweet spot between mainstream beers and imported Guinness — ceased to be relevant when measured against demand.

Richard's reluctance to bump up the price went against Hormann's and Berry's business sense: they knew the brewery could afford a price hike — that it wouldn't put off customers — and Berry wanted to ensure the shareholders got a decent dividend. He could achieve that by putting up the price per bottle by five cents.

When Richard dug in his heels, Hormann said the message was clear: 'You make lots of beer, but there's not a big pile of it sitting around here. What that tells you is that as soon you make it, people buy it . . . it gets sold.'

It was a simple supply–demand formula and the price increased.

Looking back, Hormann said the brewery owed a great debt to Berry for maintaining the tight grip on the reins after George died. 'He put a lot of work into the brewery. He was a bit too pedantic at times — literally looking for that last cent — but the brewery wouldn't be where it is now without Graeme.'

Not that Richard was always stymied, mind, he often got what he wanted, but only after he'd proved the benefits justified the expense. As the business grew, the hand-writing of invoices became a greater burden on Richard and he argued successfully for the business's first computer — although the budget extended only as far as a second-hand, refurbished PC.

Another source of tension for Richard stemmed from the fact he owned just 1000 shares in a business bearing his name. He held all the intellectual property and was the face of the business, yet it didn't belong to him in the legal sense. As one of the directors and the creative force, he had a strong say in how the business ran, but at other times he fulfilled a different role — an employee of Emerson's Brewing Company Ltd, and a lowly paid employee at that. In 2004, he earned $50,000 — well above the national median at the time, but not a fair reflection of the hours he worked and the fact the business carrying his name had become increasingly profitable.

To recognise Richard's long, often lowly paid service to the business, the directors decided to reward him via a share restructure. The company had accrued a reasonable level of imputation tax credits over the years — money slated for dividends to shareholders. The company agreed to use those credits to give Richard 21,223 shares valued at $59,000. At the same time, other shareholders got bonus shares in proportion with what they already owned. This restructure left Richard with about 12 per cent of the company. Only Ingrid had more shares than he did, holding about 24 per cent.

'He worked incredibly hard for little reward, which was something Graeme and I were conscious about all the way through,' said Mike Hormann. 'We wanted to get him more of the business. We decided at board level to give Richard some shares in recognition for years of low pay. That had the effect of watering down other people's shares — not that they were worth a great deal of money at the time, but they had some value.'

Running parallel with the decision to increase Richard's share allocation, the business had another share issue in mind — this time to raise capital for the brewery's second move. After just five years, 9 Grange Street was already too small. The brewery was running at full speed just to stand still. The demand for Pilsner and Bookbinder meant dedicating the bulk of production to those two beers.

9 Grange Street was a beautiful brewery to work with — if I had stayed small it would have been perfect. But it was terrible for the cellar-door sales because there were only three carparks. When we moved to Wickliffe Street we had queues coming out the door — it shows what a difference it makes when you make room for the customer.

The question was whether we doubled in size to a 2500-litre plant or 5000-litre plant. We made a decision to go to 5000 litres and again Farra built that. It was one of the few times we borrowed money — previous moves had been done with cash and extending our overdraft. But Wickliffe Street was a different one — we did a shareholder issue to put more money into the business as well as borrowing money from the National Bank.

While Richard thought 9 Grange Street was close to the perfect brewery — the perfection lasted only as long as the concept of 'micro' applied. By the middle of the first decade of the new century Emerson's had been at the forefront of a revolution, along with the likes of Tuatara and Epic, where the word 'micro' ceased to be applicable.

The second iteration of Emerson's brewing at 9 Grange Street, Dunedin. Photo by Geoff Griggs.

RICHARD EMERSON
THE HOPFATHER **164**

These breweries built market momentum, creating a rising wave of 'craft' beer that meant staying small — while an option — wouldn't satisfy the growing army of customers demanding more and more great-tasting beer.

'We kept running out of space,' Hormann said. His SetPoint offices had already moved from Grange Street to nearby Frederick St and again — as had been the story at Grange Street — Emerson's encroached on SetPoint space. 'At one stage, we had a storage area that Richard was using to store barrels of his whisky porter. It was an amazing experience to walk in on Monday morning after it had been shut up for a couple of days over the weekend — it smelled divine.'

But it was also symbolic of the fact Emerson's needed to move — again. To get the ideal brewery space, Graeme Berry's partner Ruth Houghton and Mike Hormann put together a company to buy a commercial property at 14 Wickliffe Street, a whole 700 metres away from 9 Grange Street. 'We did it, so we could be a friendly landlord,' Hormann said, providing another example of friends paving the way for Richard to make great beer.

'When the need to move became obvious, Michael and I thought we could buy a building and at least we'd know how it would be used,' Houghton added. 'The spirit of buying the building was so the brewery could continue — we knew we probably wouldn't lose money on it, but we certainly didn't buy it as a commercial proposition.'

Having learned the lessons from the first two breweries, Hormann and Houghton made sure they bought a big building — one capable of handling continued growth — and the brewery system quadrupled from a 1200-litre brewhouse to 5000 litres. When Emerson's moved into the building in January 2005, Hormann noted, 'Richard and I stood there when it was empty and said to each other, "We'll never fill this up."'

The Wickliffe Street brewery was opened in real style, so much so that it's still talked about in admiring if somewhat hazy tones in Dunedin to this day.

We had two different kinds of openings . . . the first was a more proper, official one with Peter Chin, the Dunedin mayor. He spoke about how he knew my father and how well the brewery was doing. It was all pretty formal, so the next night was party time.

There were many bands playing, most significantly, In A Circle with David Stedman, Phil Hurring and Darren Stedman as the drummer.

The main act was The Chills and, oh boy, it was good! Another band was Operation Rolling Thunder featuring two of Jim Falconer's brothers, Adam and Rob.

The number of people that turned up was incredible — friends of staff, bar staff from around Dunedin and friends of the brewery. After all, who could resist a piss-up in a brewery!

The last band played until about 3am and I was still hanging around trying to keep an eye on things. Eventually, I felt the only way to move people out of the brewery was to literally hose them out. As the water sprayed and people slowly stumbled out of the way, I could see their minds slowly clicking that I wanted them out and the party was over.

Incredibly, we went through nearly 700 litres of beer over the two days!

Jim Falconer, who'd come on board as a labourer towards the end of the brewery's time at 9 Grange Street, said the transition to Wickliffe Street was almost overwhelming. 'At 9 Grange Street, the business felt tiny. I remember the first time we filled eight kegs of Bookbinder to send to Regional Wines & Spirits in Wellington and standing proudly by the pallet thinking we'd made it. It didn't feel like we were on the cusp of something massive. Moving into Wickliffe Street — the building felt huge, a massive amount of space — and I wondered how we'd fill it, but it just went gangbusters.'

I had a fuck-up when we first moved into Wickliffe Street. I'd brewed for three months non-stop, seven days a week at Grange Street to fill up all the tanks in Wickliffe Street, so we had enough beer to see us through the move over the summer. When we got into Wickliffe Street, I got a new auger for malt — I put malt into the hopper and nothing happened. No malt was coming out.

I rang up the engineers and said no malt is coming out, they said put more in. I told them it was full. It turned out the auger blade was too small for the tube, so the malt was falling back into the hopper.

We needed to start making beer as all the stock was running down over Christmas. And the engineers said, 'We can't do anything about it until we come back from our holiday at the end of January.' And I was saying I've got a brewery to run, I have to make bloody beer. What was I going to do?

Suddenly I realised I had a little hand-mill from home-brewing days. We'd spend five hours in the morning crushing a tonne of grain, which we had to carry a sack at a time up the stairs to get it in the mash tun. We had to do a number of brews like that, but we had to do it to stay in business. When we got the auger fixed it took 45 minutes to crush the grist for Bookbinder.

Richard might have been on to his third brewery in 13 years when he moved into 14 Wickliffe Street, but the incident with the auger proved he was just one broken piece of equipment away from seeing his business stumble. Once the broken auger was fixed and brewing returned to schedule, the increased space at Wickliffe Street saw production ramp up considerably.

The benefits of Wickliffe Street became immediately apparent — cellar-door sales went through the roof. The reason for that had nothing to do with the brewery itself, but more its location. Wickliffe Sreet had all-day free parking, but was close enough to the city for workers to park and walk to work. Grabbing a flagon of Emerson's on the way home became a natural part of their day. At peak times in the summer, the demand for flagon-filling literally meant all hands on deck to deal with queues snaking out the door, while at Christmas time the brewery hired a specialist flagon-runner.

WHAT HAD STARTED AS A ONE-MAN BAND HAD BECOME AN ENSEMBLE AND RICHARD BEGAN TO STRUGGLE WITH THE ROLE OF BAND LEADER, SONG-WRITER, LEAD GUITARIST, PUBLICIST AND PRODUCER.

To pay for the new brewhouse, new fermenters to handle the extra production and other equipment, the company went to the shareholders to raise $400,000.

The shareholders had the option to purchase new shares in proportion to their current holding, paying $2.25 per share.

Ingrid Emerson was unhappy at her allotment of around 40,000 shares valued at just over $90,000. She had more money — from George's life insurance — and wanted to invest it, but the company regulations prevented it. Her handwritten letter to the board shows she was prepared to invest

Another fermenter goes into Wickliffe Street.

another $45,000 and she felt stymied at being unable to give the Emerson family more ownership. She also loaned money to Richard so he could maintain his shareholding, by buying up his full allotment. 'I was furious. I thought, "It's our brewery, I've got the money, why can I not put it into the brewery? Why can't we own more of it?"'

But the simple fact remained: an array of people owned Emerson's and that diverse shareholding reflected an unassailable fact: the day-to-day running of the business had slowly become too big for Richard. What had started as a one-man band had become an ensemble and Richard began to struggle with the role of band leader, song-writer, lead guitarist, publicist and producer.

Chris O'Leary's arrival at Emerson's in 2006 was timely. With his Irish surname, O'Leary earned the nickname Paddy when he worked at Roosters Brewhouse in Hastings. The moniker provided an easy way to separate him from Chris Harrison, who owned the brewpub.

Richard preferred to call him Father O'Leary. The appellation has stayed with O'Leary for around 20 years and says much about his relationship with Richard — they are tight friends and co-workers. While

O'Leary is around the same age as Richard, he is also something of a father figure. He's a minder, a colleague, a friend and a set of ears tuned to the hearing world to fill in the gaps that come with Richard's deafness. In some ways, he's stepped into the boots George left behind.

As well as bringing all of this to the table, Chris provided a much-needed gap between Richard and the brewery's growing number of staff. When the brewery consisted of Richard and a handful of colleagues, managing them proved simple enough, but larger staff numbers put an increasing demand on Richard's communication skills. Conversations that should be straightforward became complex and time-consuming, and Richard struggled with the demands of a modern workplace.

As production manager — or head brewer — O'Leary took over the day-to-day running of the operation, taking a load off Richard. More importantly, he provided Richard with the father-figure role he missed. Chris understood that, despite his ability to read lips and understand body language, Richard still needed, or wanted, someone to interact with the world on his behalf, more so when tiredness got the better of him or he had to deal with hard-to-read faces.

O'Leary didn't start life in beer — he studied forestry at the University of Canterbury. 'I was on the chainsaw for a number of years and then got into management. What I loved about forestry was the physical labour. I didn't like managing forestry workers, shoving their rates down, making them produce lots of timber for less money — it didn't feel right.'

O'Leary saw the danger in forestry, from the back-breaking nature of the labour to the life-threatening incidents that plague the industry. He figured things could be done better and became New Zealand's first forestry ergonomist. He got his Master's degree in ergonomics at Loughborough University, in Leicestershire, England, before returning home to work for Carter Holt in Hawke's Bay.

He brought home not only a Master's degree, but also a new-found appreciation for beer — notably European styles such as German Hefeweizen and Belgian Witbier. Unable to find such beers back home in New Zealand and turned off by the 'brown lagers' on tap in New Zealand, he started brewing his own.

The home-brew journey took him to Roosters Brewhouse where he happily did unpaid brewing work in order to learn more about his new passion.

His life changed when Carter Holt decided to send him to Auckland, where a position had opened up. Within a day of being offered the job he quit. He and his wife Aggie had just bought a house and were expecting their first child; they didn't want to move to Auckland, so O'Leary moved out of forestry altogether.

That night he walked into Roosters and told Harrison he'd quit his job. 'He said, "You're mad but . . . do you want to work for me?" I thought I'd be there for six months, but it became five years and Chris taught me the

Chris O'Leary became a father figure for Richard.

whole technical and business side of running a brewery. At a brewpub you learn everything from raw materials right through to the tap. I brewed three times a week and learned fast how to put out quality beer in big volume.'

O'Leary became well enough ensconced in the industry to have heard about a small brewery in Dunedin making the kind of beer he'd fallen in love with — classic European styles largely unavailable elsewhere in New Zealand.

On a holiday to Oamaru to visit Aggie's family in 1997, O'Leary took the opportunity to call in on Richard Emerson. 'Richard was a legend among home brewers and those who were starting out — it wasn't because he was deaf, but because the beers were stunning and quite edgy back in those days. While we were in Oamaru with the in-laws I told Aggie I wanted to meet this guy, so I said, "I'm going down to Dunedin for the day to visit Richard."'

The first time Chris came to the brewery in Dunedin, the phone rang. I said, 'Chris, can you answer the phone? I don't usually get people to do this, but you're here.'

It was an unusual phone call from Australia. They wanted to know if I was prepared to come over to Australia to pick up a significant prize from their beer awards. Chris was quite shocked to be part of that process, telling me that I'd won a trophy for the Weissbier.

The organisers of the Australian International Beer Awards wanted Richard to come to Melbourne to receive his first major trophy. Richard had no spare cash to pay for airfares and accommodation, and his parents were overseas on holiday so he couldn't ask them for money. Alistair Smillie, a director of Emerson's, stepped up and brokered a deal with the National Bank to sponsor one of their customers. The sponsorship for the trip totalled a princely $778. That such a slender sum couldn't be found for such a momentous occasion illustrates the tight nature of the brewery's finances. The three-piece suit Richard wore to the awards came from the Salvation Army store. 'Someone had died in it but that was okay — it looked brand new.'

When Richard's parents arrived home from their overseas holiday soon afterwards, Richard went to the airport to pick them up and told them they had to divert past the brewery to pick up batteries for a hearing aid that he'd left there. 'We said it was okay, but really we wanted to get home,'

Ingrid remembered. 'And when we got to the brewery everybody was there. In our absence, Richard had won a trophy for Weissbier in Australia and this was the celebration — we couldn't believe it.'

After that phone call, the friendship between Chris and Richard grew, built on beer, sausages . . . and faxes.

Chris would come down every few months and we'd brew a beer together and we became very good friends. On another visit, we arranged to get some Weissbier sausages to eat with the Weissbier, but we started drinking a bit too early and got hungry. We decided the best way to cook the sausages was in the electric jug — to boil the sausages in there. It seems like a crazy thing to do, but I can only explain it by saying we are both very passionate and we wanted to get on with it and it was the only way to cook them. The kettle would boil over and switch itself off, and we'd turn it on again until they were done. The coffee in the brewery tasted like sausages for a long time. It took weeks to get the smell out of the jug and remove all the fat.

The pair communicated by sending hand-scrawled faxes back and forth between Hastings and Dunedin. They routinely sat in front of their respective televisions — Richard's with closed captions — a beer at hand, watching *Planes and Automobiles* with Robbie Coltrane, and sending faxed sheets of commentary to and fro.

The pair became early adopters of ICQ, one of the first internet-based instant message services that paved the way for Facebook Messenger, WhatsApp and other similar tools. 'When we got ICQ, we'd communicate daily for many years from the late nineties to the early 2000s,' O'Leary said. 'Then Nokia put out a special phone that they offered at a discount to deaf people — the Nokia Communicator — and you could call and fax from the phone. For Richard it was a game-changer.'

After learning the ropes at Roosters, O'Leary thought he had enough knowledge to go out on his own, so he set up Limburg Brewery. He brewed his beer at Roosters on his days off, making a signature Belgian Witbier (a wheat beer with coriander and orange peel) sold through Regional Wines & Spirits in Wellington.

'Chris Harrison had capped my salary as he couldn't afford to pay me any more — that's why he let me brew on the weekends, but it got to the point where he said, "You might have to go out on your own."'

Using his house as leverage and drawing on an investment from his parents, O'Leary gambled on making a success of his small regional brewery the way Richard had with Emerson's. While aficionados still talk about Limburg beers in reverential tones, for various reasons unrelated to the beer, the business model didn't work.

'We started running out of money and the house was on the line. I had a shareholder who owned pubs — he kept saying, "Don't worry about making a profit, focus on building a brand and one day Lion will buy you." We borrowed more money from the bank to further invest in the brand. Richard was supportive and encouraging me, saying work with what you've got, don't get ahead of yourself.'

Unlike Emerson's — with George's tight fiscal control ensuring growth came from cash flow — Limburg's became heavily indebted. The business took on another shareholder, Craig Cooper, who today owns Bach Brewing. A restructure followed, but the money didn't flow as freely as the beer and, at the bank's suggestion, the business went into liquidation.

'ANZ bank was brilliant and said the best thing we can do is call in the loan and see if your business partners will back it. If the partners come up with the money you'll be fine; if they don't you'll lose your house, but you can untangle yourself from this situation and get out of the mess you have got into. We went into liquidation. We lost the house.'

Chris and Aggie had $5000 to their name after selling their Morris Minor van to a collector — at the time it was the oldest running vehicle of its type in the world. Chris had job offers from Mac's waterfront brewery in Wellington and from Emerson's. Richard's pay offer was a lot less and Dunedin was further away, but Chris didn't hesitate.

Before George had died, he and Richard had often talked about Chris coming to Emerson's, but George always nixed the idea, saying the two couldn't work together because they would clash.

'George was right — our two egos would have clashed,' Chris said. 'But after the humbling time I'd been through, I wanted to focus on my family. In negotiating my contract with Emerson's, I said, "I don't want to front the business or go to trade shows — Richard is the front of the business, I just want to brew."'

'I was stressed because of the business failing and I was drinking heavily at the time — it wasn't good for our family. We decided to come to Dunedin because it felt like a much better place to bring up a family and we've never regretted it — Dunedin was the best thing to have happened to us. The city has been good to me; it's the best place in the world to raise a family and the kids, and my family life, just blossomed. And working with Richard has created a sense of family too — being part of something and being included. I'd been through a rough time, but I came here to a sense of belonging with Emerson's and Dunedin, which was such a nice place to be, compared with where we'd come from. And I got to work with my best friend — you couldn't have asked for anything more — everything lined up to make us happy.'

While Chris insisted that he didn't want to be out the front of the business or going to trade shows, his closeness to and understanding of Richard meant that he often found himself helping out at these events.

One of the pitfalls in lip-reading is discovering that someone is already talking to me and I swing my head around to read their lips, but the critical first few words have been missed. That makes working out the context of the sentence even harder: was it a directive or a question? Many times I would have to ask the person to repeat the sentence to harvest the information, so I could ensure I got the context right.

Lip-reading a group is even more challenging, as it's even harder to grasp the subject of the conversation before letting my mind go forth with information to add to the conversation. I'll never forgot the look on my mates' faces at an Indian restaurant when I had been trying hard to follow the dialogue going on with a group of half-a-dozen of them, picking up key words here and there. I swore they were talking about poppadums, given we were sitting in an Indian restaurant that made sense, so I piped up that 'I liked the flavoured ones and the ones they have here have a good texture . . .'

My friends stopped talking, mouths open, silent for a moment then burst out laughing. I couldn't figure out why my comment was that funny until someone commented that they had changed conversation topic and were talking about condoms! Aaaargh!

My mates could see the lighter side of things and this does show how difficult it is to follow a conversation and the danger of the topic changing just when you think you have it sussed.

As a result of misunderstandings like the poppadum–condom mix-up, Richard often compensates for the risk of losing the thread by taking charge

BOOKBINDER

While London Porter launched Emerson's, the beer that helped the growth of the business came in the form of a 3.7 per cent English-style bitter, distinguished by the use of New Zealand hops, all created from a recipe scribbled on the back of an envelope. Bookbinder, or Bookie as it's affectionately known, was launched at the annual Victoria Fete in Oamaru, where Richard wanted a lower-alcohol 'session' beer to go alongside London Porter and 1812. He wanted to make what he called 'a four-pinter beer, low in alcohol compared with London Porter and 1812'. He wrote the recipe on the back of an envelope the night before he made it, aiming to create a beer that was juicy and refreshing. 'I used a touch of black malt to change the pH and the colour. I used some New Zealand hops and it was just what I was looking for.' The name Bookbinder comes from the fact Richard has two friends who are both bookbinders by trade — high school friend David Stedman and Michael O'Brien from Oamaru, who now brews his own beer under the Craftwork label alongside partner Lee-Anne Scotti.

of the conversation and steering it to safe ground. This habit annoyed George who would admonish his son, saying, 'Richard! You need to listen! You're not listening.'

And some days, that's exactly what he prefers to do. When tired, or surrounded by too much background noise, Richard finds communication difficult and has become adept at pretending not to understand or even avoiding eye contact altogether to avoid being dragged into conversation destined to go in circles.

Chris remembers one beer festival where Richard stood at the Emerson's stand with Jim Falconer. When a punter walked up to them and said, 'I understand Richard Emerson's here, I'd love to meet him,' Richard pointed to Jim and said, 'That's him!' and promptly wandered off.

On the flipside, Richard often understands far more than he 'hears'. At an event at The Malthouse bar in Wellington, a variety of brewers — including Chris — played host to a debate on various issues in the industry. At the end of it, members of the audience had a chance to ask questions.

From his spot on the podium, Chris could see Richard seated in the front row of the audience facing the panel, so he could read the conversation. Part of the debate had been about the difference between kegged beer and bottled beer. In those days Bookbinder came as a keg-only beer and hadn't yet been put into bottles — despite growing demand for it.

Someone at the back of the room asked a question about bottled Bookbinder. Before anyone could answer, Richard stood, turned to face the audience and said, 'The reason Bookbinder is not in the bottle is . . .'

'People were absolutely astounded,' O'Leary said. 'And I said, "There it is, people, Richard has been having you on all these years — he's not deaf at all!"'

It stands as an example of Richard's skill in judging the course of the conversation — he'd followed the panellists and figured where it might head. He'd heard the question about Bookbinder in bottles so many times in the past, he'd braced himself for the question and as soon as he thought he heard the word 'Bookbinder' he jumped to his feet to answer.

Lip-reading is not always so straightforward, however, and often comes with hazards attached. For most people, walking and talking at the same time provides little difficulty. Not so for Richard, with friends losing count of the number of times he's walked into lamp-posts, parking meters, signs or other obstructions because his head is turned to watch the faces of those walking beside him.

CHAPTER

A WEDDING, A DEATH AND PLENTY OF DRAMA

One day, I broke my foot by kicking a keg because I was so frustrated at one of the staff. They were swearing at me; I felt I was being attacked and my integrity was being undermined. I had to leave the room because I was so frustrated and I went out and whack! I kicked the keg.

Richard and Norma on their wedding day at Bannockburn, Central Otago, with Norma's daughter, Frances, and Richard's mother, Ingrid.

I went into the office and was complaining about how much it hurt. Chris told me, 'It's not broken. Don't be so stupid.' But I went down to accident and emergency, and it turned out it was broken.

Soon afterwards, I had to fly up to Wellington, and I said to Chris I'm a bit worried about getting deep vein thrombosis. Chris again said, 'Don't be so stupid. You won't get deep vein thrombosis. Just get on the plane, and stop being a dick.'

The next thing, Chris gets a text from me: 'You won't guess where I am, I'm in hospital with a blood clot. On warfarin.' The doctor said, 'You can't drink when you're on warfarin.' And I said, 'But I've got a brewery! I have to do quality control.'

I did some more research online and discovered that I could have one pint a day. Chris was livid. He said that's seven pints a week and not even he has that much.

Everyone who knows Richard knows that drama follows him like a loyal dog. He seems to pull chaos out of the air. Even if it's not a major drama, a conversation with Richard Emerson will be filled with table thumping, waving hands, shouts of joy or frustration — he's a physical, animated, robust character.

The high energy and sense of boundless adventure that defined his boyhood and carried him through the first 15 years of Emerson's remained, but as the brewery continued to grow and staff numbers increased, the burden on Richard started to stretch him.

Jim Falconer, who'd progressed from being a labourer doing 'donkey work' to a brewing role, described Richard in the early days of Wickliffe Street as 'manic, a whirlwind — he just did everything and he had so much energy'.

All that energy coupled with his sense of responsibility meant Richard tried to do too much. He'd always been a person prone to frustration — at not being understood, at being unable to understand some people, at not knowing how to pronounce a word he'd never seen before, at missing out on things that others took for granted. Add to that the frustration of being deaf and trying to run a large business — it was just exhausting.

'Richard gets very tired,' Chris O'Leary said. 'That comes from late nights championing the brand, and constantly having to work to understand people really tires him out. He's like an Energizer Bunny — he goes and goes and then crashes.'

With Chris on board and looking after the brewing side of the operation, Richard could retreat from that aspect of the business, but the reduction in brewing work was more than overtaken by other roles. As the face of an increasingly well-known brand, Richard often travelled to events around the country such as tastings and festivals as part of the company's marketing strategy.

He also began to play less of a management role. By his own admission, Richard struggled with people management. He'd gone from working on his own, with family and friends helping, to having one, two and then a handful of staff. But at Wickliffe Street the staff numbers — and the associated issues — had grown to a point where his usual practice of talking to people one-on-one became too time-consuming and increasingly fraught. When it came to discussing personal matters, for instance, Richard's disability made it difficult for both him and his staff to deal with issues as a normal business might.

EVERYONE WHO KNOWS RICHARD KNOWS THAT DRAMA FOLLOWS HIM LIKE A LOYAL DOG. HE SEEMS TO PULL CHAOS OUT OF THE AIR.

Graeme Berry could see all this and decided the time had come for him to step aside from his de facto management role and hire a professional manager. After years of loyal service to George and the brewery, he retired and Bob King came in as manager.

Bob became integral to the business, but not without the teething problems associated with the unusual dynamic at Emerson's, which required him to do what many others had found impossible: manage Richard. 'People were reverential towards him — they were evangelical in their devotion and commitment to the beers. It was like a cult for some people who had followed the brand from the early days. And Richard was the brand. But he wasn't the majority shareholder — many people didn't realise that. As general manager, you're there with a founder who's also an employee — it was a difficult balancing act and led to reasonably robust discussions about things.'

The other area of dramatic change came with Chris O'Leary providing technical expertise to the operation that complemented Richard's passion and understanding of flavours. For all his science background, Richard had succeeded to that point because he knew what worked flavour-wise, but as Chris soon discovered, technical issues occasionally impacted on the consistency of the beer.

O'Leary noted the Pilsner, for instance, had a signature fruity flavour note that came from the yeast being under stress and throwing off a fruit ester that, while complementary to the flavour profile of the hops, should not have been there.

The issue didn't cause any problems because the beer had plenty of time to condition — that is, to sit in tanks for a few weeks before it was sold. 'Beers clean up over time when they are brewed by people who understand the process, but as the Pilsner became more popular, we had to turn it around more quickly. We no longer had the luxury of that time. So we had to

Chris O'Leary, left, became Richard's right-hand man at Emerson's.

make sure everything about the brew was right — we needed a more healthy ferment, which meant putting in enough yeast, giving it enough oxygen — so it lost some of those stressed esters that gave the Pilsner its signature aroma people loved. The flavours changed but it was better brewed.'

Since day one, Richard had used whole hops in his brewing rather than the dehydrated pellets widely used in most big breweries. There's a shedload of extra work that comes from using whole hops as they soak up so much water, making it an unenviable and quite physical task to dig them out of a kettle after a brew. The brewery could handle the extra labour required for that when it was small. The brewers had developed a habit of leaving the hops in the kettle overnight to let them dry out as much as possible to make the digging easier, but increased production meant brewing every day instead of every second day, and that in turn meant the hops needed digging out the same day to have the kettle ready for the following morning's brew. That forced a pragmatic switch to pelletised hops, which are much easier to dig out.

Around the same time, the Pilsner went from organic to non-organic. 'We couldn't get enough organic Riwaka hops, so we chose to maintain the flavour by using as much organic as we could and supplementing it with non-organic,' O'Leary said. 'The passion was for maintaining the flavour rather than trying to stay organic.'

Richard also used to brew Bookbinder in an open fermenter in the traditional English style, but that open fermenter could no longer handle all the Bookbinder they needed to brew. O'Leary moved the fermentation to a modern conical tank and the 'geography' of that tank had the effect of cleaning up the beer as it no longer sat on a large surface area of yeast, picking up some of the yeast's flavour characteristics along the way. Instead of a volatile, fast fermentation in the open fermenter, the beer moved to a temperature-controlled environment. The process took longer, but resulted in a cleaner-tasting beer with a longer shelf life and fewer volatile aromas.

These moves represented big changes from the brewery's perspective and while the integrity of Richard's beers hadn't changed — if anything they improved dramatically — some people started to notice that the products tasted different. That didn't impact on sales though, as the market continued to drink every batch of Emerson's as fast as it could be produced. Even when the odd problem surfaced and a query or complaint found its way back to the brewery, it was a moot point — the beer had gone.

One serious issue did have the potential to derail the business, however. At the end of one summer, a batch of Old 95 — an aged ale — had started to gush on opening, a sure sign a bug had crept into the system somewhere. The Old 95 had been stored high up in the warehouse where it was exposed to heat over the course of the summer allowing whatever had infected the beer to make itself known.

Chris raised the issue with Richard, saying, 'Something's not right.'

'I was shitting myself — I'd only been there six months and was worried I'd wrecked a key beer. I sent the samples off for testing at the food science department at Otago University. A week later they came back with a plastic bag of agar plates they'd grown. They took out these plates, which had all these cultures growing on them. "What's growing?" I asked. "Everything." "Everything?" "Everything you can think of is growing." Holy shit.

'They suggested I go back through the process to find the source of this bacteria. I started with the bottling line, pulling it apart, and it didn't take long to find this long piece of pink snot connected to the internal mechanism. The entire bottle-filling machine was filled with gunk. Everything was going through that machine — all our beers — but what saved us was the fact that back in those days the beer was drunk so fast there was not enough time for anything to grow. But the Old 95 had been aged and had gotten warm, so that had given the bugs time to grow.'

Once the machine had been cleaned, Chris had to find out how the bugs had burrowed their way into the system. He asked Richard if he had any clues. 'Hmmm,' said Richard, 'I think I know.'

It turns out Richard — for all his great brewing nous — had made a fundamental error when bottling a porter that had been aged in whisky barrels. He'd pumped directly from the barrels into the bottling machine. Wooden barrels are notorious for being full of bacteria — it's a quality that helps create sour beers — but it's not something any brewery wants in its bottling line.

It was another sign that Richard had too much on his plate and it proved how critical it was to have the technical skills O'Leary brought to the business.

The biggest force for Richard's success had always been his palate and his understanding of flavour and where it comes from — these combined with Chris's technical ability were critical to Emerson's evolution from a boutique brewery to a true powerhouse of the industry. 'Chris is like a brother to me and having him come along helped me with running the business. Between the two of us — it was a good partnership.'

Like any 'brother', Chris looked out for Richard's best interests. His arrival at Emerson's in Dunedin coincided with Richard's slow break-up with Marian, and it didn't take long for Chris to play an instrumental role in setting up his friend on a blind date.

Chris was visiting his sister-in-law Josie in Christchurch, and she was saying a lot of Christchurch women she knew were lamenting the lack of good-quality men in the city. Chris being Chris said, 'Who do you know who is looking?' and asked Josie to list the qualities of women who were looking for men. One of them was a former broadcaster from South Africa and Chris thought I'd be interested, so he got her number.

A little while later, I was in Christchurch doing a beer dinner and I was just finishing, so I texted this woman, saying, 'Hi, this is Richard Emerson — a friend of Josie's — would you like to join me for a drink?'

She replied saying she had a daughter and couldn't go out at such short notice. So I said, 'You name a place for coffee tomorrow and I'll be there.'

She was able to choose her own comfort ground and I met her at a café near the Christchurch Casino the next day. It was only meant to be a quick coffee, but it turned into more than an hour-and-a-half-long chat. I was quite taken by her. There was something that attracted me to her right away — there was a personal chemistry that I could smell. I kept thinking, 'I love that smell; there's something about her I like.'

We communicated by text a lot. At one point, my accountant Robyn drew my attention to the fact that my phone bill was getting high because there were 6000 texts one month . . . I didn't worry about the cost, brushed it under the carpet.

We'd visit each other every weekend. It started being the case that on Fridays, I would say to Chris, 'Well, Father, there's not much to do around the brewery on a Friday afternoon. I suppose I could head up to Christchurch.' So around one o'clock, I'd jump in the car and zoom up to Christchurch in time for dinner. I'd leave Christchurch at 4.30am on Monday morning to be back at the brewery to start work by 9.30.

Norma Odendaal had been through a pretty rough time when Richard Emerson contacted her with that out-of-the-blue text message.

She had worked as a journalist and TV presenter in South Africa.

In the mid-to-late 1990s as South Africa transitioned from years of apartheid she and her husband Frans van Rensburg — who worked as a radio broadcaster — felt a rise in violent crime wasn't conducive to raising children in the republic.

Norma had a son from a previous relationship, Julian, and she and Frans had a daughter, Frances. 'As a journalist, I was seeing all the stories coming through from police on crime — the situation felt really bad — and we could only report a fraction of it. We couldn't see how we could raise our children in that environment. We started looking at places to move to.'

The couple settled on New Zealand after considering Canada and Australia. They emigrated in 1997 and, after starting in Auckland, they settled in Christchurch when Norma got a job at Newstalk ZB. While they had escaped one life in South Africa, further personal trauma awaited them in their new home with both Norma and Frans diagnosed with cancer in 2001.

Norma had breast cancer and underwent a mastectomy while Frans was diagnosed with bladder cancer — untreatable with chemotherapy. He died in 2005 and Norma was left to raise two children on her own. Julian was 16 and Frances was 10.

In 2007, Norma had found work for Environment Canterbury where she met Chris O'Leary's sister-in-law. 'Josie got a visit from Chris, who asked, "Do you have someone you can introduce to Richard?" Josie gave my number to Chris and then said to me, "I hope you don't mind, I've given your number to someone."

'At that stage, I was starting to feel okay with being on my own — I certainly wasn't in the market for blind dates. Then Josie explained to me this person was deaf . . . and I thought, "Okay, I really don't have the energy to go through a blind date, let alone a blind date with a deaf person. It wasn't about the disability — I just wasn't interested.

'Then I got a text from Richard asking to meet up for a drink — it was quite late and I said, "No, I can't leave my daughter alone." Besides, I was in my pyjamas, watching TV. So Richard said how about coffee next day. Okay.

'We met at a café near Environment Canterbury and, lo and behold, we could talk! We communicated well in fact, and we had a lot in common. We started texting and emailing and then started seeing each other — not long after that Richard came up to Christchurch again and we went to Akaroa for the weekend.'

While they communicated well, Norma did have doubts about this new man in her life. 'He's got no tact, no filter, which upset me quite a lot when we first met. And he's quite a paradox — on one hand he's very self-focused, he can get accused of being selfish, but he has this amazingly generous streak too. I was thinking he's both generous and selfish — what the hell is going on?'

When Norma said they had a lot in common, the coincidences make their relationship somehow seem predestined. Her late husband Frans had — like Richard — been a steam-train enthusiast, while she and Frans both loved good beer.

———

NORMA DID HAVE DOUBTS ABOUT THIS NEW MAN IN HER LIFE. 'HE'S GOT NO TACT, NO FILTER, WHICH UPSET ME QUITE A LOT WHEN WE FIRST MET. AND HE'S QUITE A PARADOX — ON ONE HAND HE'S VERY SELF-FOCUSED, HE CAN GET ACCUSED OF BEING SELFISH, BUT HE HAS THIS AMAZINGLY GENEROUS STREAK TOO. I WAS THINKING HE'S BOTH GENEROUS AND SELFISH — WHAT THE HELL IS GOING ON?'

———

In the days of sanctions in South Africa, the local brew, Castle Lager, ruled the roost and finding alternative beer proved difficult. Norma and Frans did find one bottle store that sold imported beer. 'It was outrageously expensive, but every weekend we would go and buy a bottle of something, one each for a treat. I loved all of them — I realised beer can actually taste like something.'

When Norma and Frans moved to New Zealand, Frans struggled to find work and they had to be more frugal — and they found New Zealand craft beer too expensive — so their weekly treat became an imported beer of some description. Norma had fallen in love with Belgian beers. And when she fell in love with Richard, well, he came with his own supply of Belgian-style beers.

About the time Norma came into Richard's life, another important person left it —Professor Jean-Pierre Dufour.

Belgian-born Jean-Pierre had arrived at the University of Otago in 1995, heading up the food science faculty. He had a strong interest in brewing — particularly in yeast cell metabolism and hop characteristics — and a passion for aroma.

One of his former students, Fork & Brewer's Kelly Ryan, remembered 'JP' being so sensitive to garlic, he once stopped a lecture, saying he couldn't concentrate because someone in the room had eaten garlic for lunch. The culprits — a group who'd had a curry for lunch — admitted as much and were ejected from the lecture theatre.

Dufour authored or co-authored papers on a range of subjects from how yeast can give beer a fruity character; identifying odour compounds in coriander; the assessment of different storage conditions on fresh salmon; how different essential oils affect hop aroma; and the characteristics of fresh bread aromas and how they affect consumers.

Richard's love of aroma and flavour drew him to JP's work and they built a strong relationship around Emerson's beer. So much so that when JP was giving a lecture entitled 'You, Louis Pasteur: 120 years of brewing science', he asked Richard if he would be happy to supply the beer for it.

When Dad was still around, we heard there was going to be a new professor at the food science department at the university and that he was from Belgium. He'd heard about my brewery — I don't know how — and he asked for our beer to be poured for his inaugural lecture, which was all about yeast.

It was a great lecture — he had an image of an animal representing the yeast. It was sucking in the liquid sugar, the wort, and it was farting CO_2 and pissing ethanol. He tried to explain that just as each animal had its own personal odour, that was what the yeast contributed to the flavour of the beer — its personal odour.

After that I got to know him more — he was invited along as a judge for the New Zealand Beer Awards and I always tried to spend time with him. I love Belgian beers and I wanted to learn about Belgian yeast strains.

Working with JP after that lecture, Richard made a 1200-litre brew of a Belgian Tripel, fermented in 120-litre batches with 10 different yeasts to see how each would react. It took Richard back to the way he'd tested different yeasts when home brewing, and together the two men rated all the beers. 'I remember one of them smelt like PVA glue, which wasn't very good. We tried them again as they got older and it was quite clear some were better than others — JP was keen to use all those beers to teach students about the flavour and aroma of different yeasts.'

After Otago, JP went to Ghana to try to improve the quality and techniques used in the production of sorghum beer in Africa. He died suddenly while attending a conference in Nigeria in 2007, at the age of just 54, leaving both Richard and many others in the New Zealand beer scene devastated. To this day, Emerson's makes a JP beer, which is released on 2 June each year to mark the professor's birthday.

JP was only in my life for a short time, but he had a big impact on me — I loved being able to talk to a professor about flavour. I was devastated, so I thought, as a way to honour JP, we'd take the best Belgian Tripel from those trial batches I'd done and make a beer in his honour. I also took fifty cents from the sale of each bottle and put it into a fund for the JP Scholarship.

After seven years of making JP, we built up quite a fund, but the university didn't want anything to do with alcohol sponsorship. I was frustrated at this namby-pamby political correctness, so we worked outside the university by sponsoring the students directly. We've sponsored five students. The latest one was a carry-over of the previous project working on the relationship between yeast and hops.

I'm a firm believer that yeast affects hop-flavour outcome. Some breweries say they don't like using a particular hop, but I think it could be that their house yeast doesn't bring out the flavour attribute they are looking for in the hops. We are seeing some evidence that fermentation has influence on hops flavours, but we need more research to make it clear. You can brew the same beer with two different yeasts and it changes the hop profile completely.

In 2009, Norma became a New Zealand citizen and, with her daughter, she moved to Dunedin to take up a role with AgResearch at Invermay.

In September that year, Richard and Norma had planned a trip to South Africa, so he could meet her parents. In May, they decided to get married first and make the South Africa trip their honeymoon — but that meant some rushing around before the nuptials on 22 August.

First, Richard had to get divorced from Marian with all the legalities and paperwork that entailed. Only then could they plan the wedding day.

'We thought it was too late to formally invite people to our wedding, so we decided to just send a notice out to our friends and family saying that we were getting married,' Norma said. 'In the letter, we acknowledged that it was late notice and that we did not expect them to be there, but that we would welcome them if they decide to come.' Unfortunately, Norma's son Julian couldn't attend as he was doing his army training.

Around 20 people crammed into a 'tiny but lovely' church in the Central Otago wine-making town of Bannockburn for the ceremony. There, Richard had everyone in stitches with his typical impatience. 'I remember being in the church and the minister just kept talking and talking, and eventually I interrupted to say, "Look, can I kiss my wife?'

A lunch at the Mt Difficulty winery ran well into the evening, as did a later party at the Wickliffe Street brewery put on for all those who couldn't attend the Bannockburn celebration.

Just days after the wedding, and before they flew to South Africa, Richard claimed the most coveted prize in the New Zealand beer scene, with Emerson's named Champion Brewery at the annual beer awards.

The occasion became more memorable — and immortalised — when friends spotted that Richard had turned up for the awards in Wellington wearing two different shoes.

On the morning of the awards, he'd woken in the dark in Dunedin, got dressed and travelled to Wellington wearing one brown shoe and one green shoe. Perhaps because he spends so much time looking at people's faces, he didn't notice the error during the day, and his travelling companion, Chris O'Leary, resisted the urge to set him straight — there was too much fun to be had from watching the comedy unfold.

When Richard found out during the awards dinner, he responded in a typically relaxed and self-effacing manner: 'Oh well, at least I'm wearing one shoe from each of my favourite pairs.'

Not long after Richard and Norma had married, Richard's tendency to sometimes get the wrong end of the conversational stick came back to bite him. Over a few drinks with Chris and Aggie, someone asked the question: if you could leave your partner for one night only, to have an affair, who

would you pick? Richard misheard the question and blurted out 'Percy Montgomery' — the South African rugby fullback of the time.

Naturally, this didn't fall under the old adage of 'what happens on tour stays on tour' as Richard later found out when he was stopped by a traffic cop near Palmerston.

I saw the flashing blue lights and pulled over. When the cop came up, I said, 'Is there a problem, sir?' I was pretty sure I hadn't been speeding. I couldn't understand what he was saying — he was a grumpy old cop and it was just 'blah, blah, blah' but he was pointing to the front of my car. I thought, 'Have I hit something and not noticed?' I got out and walked around the front where he was pointing and there was a cardboard sign taped to the front bumper that said: 'I Love Percy'. My fucking workmates . . .

Richard and Norma were married in 2009 – the same year Emerson's was crowned New Zealand's champion brewery.

While settling into married life, Richard began to hatch another life-changing plan. All his life he'd been consumed by Central Otago Railway — those train-photographing trips with his father had built it into his DNA and now the time felt right to live a dream of moving to the country. With the brewery humming along with Bob King as manager and Chris O'Leary overseeing production, Richard no longer needed to be there for hours on end as he had in the past when he was brewer, manager, marketer and quality controller.

He had an eye for Middlemarch, which had become a busy country town in summer thanks to its destination as the start — or end — of the increasingly popular Otago Central Rail Trail. Richard had no qualms about making the one-hour commute to and from Dunedin.

'Richard pulled us towards Middlemarch,' Norma said. 'He's a sentimental person and feels really connected to the railway line because of his dad. I liked the idea of moving away from the city to the countryside.'

They bought the Middlemarch house in October 2010, but didn't move there permanently until 2011. Norma's daughter Frances, now 14, continued to go to school in Dunedin and would travel into the city with Richard each morning and home again after he finished work. Frances later started working at the brewery in the afternoons, filling bottles and running errands.

Apart from convincing Norma to move to a small rural town when she'd already downsized cities from Christchurch to Dunedin, he also needed to borrow money from his business for a deposit on a home. He presented his case to the board of directors, telling them he wanted to buy a house. The directors were happy to advance the money, but Richard, rather cheekily, omitted to tell them the location of his dream home.

Once the sale went through, it raised a few eyebrows among the directors for two reasons: Richard's distance from the brewery and the cost of the commute — given he now planned to drive roughly 800 kilometres a week in his company vehicle. The petrol costs alone would put a large dent in the ledger.

Norma quickly built a life in Middlemarch. She's on the local community board and has opened a café called Tap & Dough, serving pizza and beer to hungry and thirsty rail-trail riders.

'In 2017, we did the rail-trail trip and every town had great pubs, great food. We met up with other rail trailers and the feeling was that Middlemarch didn't have that to the same degree. There was a café-bar, but it wasn't open many nights a week and then it closed.'

Norma and Richard decided to take over the lease at what used to be Quench. 'It's not going to be a great money-maker. It sounds altruistic but it's not a lie — we thought we can't let this happen to Middlemarch. The town wasn't getting people stopping because it lacked venues for having a meal and a drink outside the pub. For rail-trail providers, there wasn't an incentive to book people in Middlemarch.'

After the shift to Middlemarch, Richard had to start contemplating another move. The Wickliffe Street brewery he thought would be his last proved too small almost from the day it opened. Staff numbers had grown, production had increased and, by 2009, it became clear production would outpace capacity in the near, rather than distant, future.

As Jim Falconer noted, almost from day one, 'the HIAB trucks kept coming, dropping off more tanks, and they didn't stop'.

Some of this is captured in a SWOT — strengths, weaknesses, opportunities and threats — analysis exercise Richard did in 2008. His handwritten notes record the weaknesses the brewery faced, including 'Richard's management skills'.

Threats came from the global financial crisis of the time, and a number of emerging rival 'microbreweries'.

His strategy remained continuing to build the business a 'pint at a time' through customer loyalty and targeting 'small, funky, local bars'.

The brand promised 'A reliable sensory experience'.

Richard created what he called his big, hairy, audacious goal: 'to be the best regional brewery in New Zealand with the most respected, reliable brand, and to be known for innovative beers and ideas'. Later, he appended that goal with another note: 'To be the most sought-after craft beer in Australasia.'

In many ways, he'd already gone a long way to achieving that goal because Emerson's had arguably become the best regional brewery in the country and it definitely produced some of the most respected and innovative beers on the shelves. And at that stage, whether Richard knew it or not, he had something that others coveted — his beer (and more so the brewery) had already become one of the most 'sought-after' in Australasia.

SALE OF THE CENTURY

A quite significant factor in selling the business was that as it grew it became harder for me to manage. I couldn't talk about employment issues — I couldn't talk over the phone — I still had to go and see people personally. Other people could deal with issues in a fraction of the time it took me, just by picking up the phone. It was frustrating for me because I couldn't just do that like a normal person could. And at Wickliffe Street, we were boxing ourselves in.

We had to grow — we couldn't ask the shareholders for more money. We'd already asked them for extra funds. How would we get the funds? How would we move forward?

That's when Lion came along. I was the only one apart from the directors who knew what was happening. All the staff were in the dark. Chris was most frustrated because he was trying to get the business going forward and I was having to say 'hang on' — I had to try to find ways of slowing him down. It was the hardest period of my life — keeping things quiet and trying to keep the business going.

When Lion came courting in 2011, Richard didn't overreact. He'd been wooed before — including by Lion's arch-rival DB, who were way ahead of the curve when they first approached Emerson's in 2004.

Others had sniffed around — Australian giant Foster's had talked long and hard about a distribution deal, as had Coca-Cola. In both cases, those giant global companies wanted to take Emerson's product and sell it through their channels. DB, through former managing director Brian Blake, noted in 2004 that they were 'very confident we can find an appropriate "go forward" path that closely aligns the market aspirations of Emerson's and the market aspirations of DB Breweries'.

Richard admitted thinking about DB's offer, 'but I never really had a feeling for DB and didn't really like their beers. I could have gone further with DB, but they only wanted a partial deal and it just didn't feel right that DB could be part of Emerson's.'

All these approaches came at a time when Emerson's experienced rapid growth despite a marketing budget that approximated . . . nothing. Sales grew on old-fashioned word of mouth and publicity from beer awards, yet one annual report noted 'we cannot produce enough beer to supply the demand'.

The approaches from multinationals such as Coke, Foster's or Heineken (through DB) couldn't solve the inherent problem Emerson's faced. All of them were talking about distribution deals — of taking Emerson's to a wider audience — but that demanded more investment in production facilities to create the beer to meet the increased demand such a deal would bring. Emerson's didn't know where that money would come from.

Even with the move to Wickliffe Street, by 2011 the brewery was flat out standing still, which brought huge pressure to bear on the key players, Richard, Chris and manager Bob King.

King almost immediately felt the growing pains against the backdrop of the company culture created under George Emerson's conservative reign — avoid debt and grow out of cash flow. 'The brewery had always done well by reinvesting cash,' and King said, 'but the new plant was out of cash flow.'

It's often hard for those outside the industry to understand how a brewery can have seemingly endless demand and yet struggle to make money, but rapid growth is often the last thing a brewery needs. Buying more ingredients and working harder and faster is not going to solve a capacity problem.

The brewery tried that — it doubled down on brew days, with two shifts introduced so beer could be produced morning and night. That's all well and good, but that beer needs to move through the system faster than previously — and that's literally move through the system, through pumps and filters and pipes of a certain width. To move more beer requires increased flow rates through pumps, bigger filtration systems, faster chilling techniques to cool beer from boiling down to around 20°C, the ideal temperature for fermentation.

If even one of the systems can't keep up, the brewery runs out of time in the day to get things done. And if the system can't work fast enough, the answer is to spend more money on big-ticket capital items such as pumps, hoses, filters and chiller plates . . . and even then, once the extra beer flows faster through the system, the brewery requires extra room to store, package and warehouse the beer before it goes to the customer.

To make beer properly takes time. Fermentation takes a few days, but then the beer needs to condition. There's a sweet spot around conditioning — rush the process and the beer might retain some sharp edges; hang on too long and it's either taking up space that can be used for another brew or it could slowly deteriorate. Some breweries move their beer quickly through the conditioning phase because demand requires it.

In an ideal world, a brewery would have enough beer in its tanks to handle a spike in demand, so they always want some on hand rather than brewing to order. And they need bright tanks for every type of beer on the go, so a brewery making four or five core beers such as Emerson's with Bookbinder, Pilsner, 1812 and London Porter, needs enough tanks for each batch. Tanks cost money and take up space.

Then the beer must be kegged or bottled. Those processes have to move fast enough to keep up with the flow from the bright tanks. If they don't, all you've done is just moved the bottleneck.

In the period leading up to Lion's approach, the Emerson's bottling line warranted a place in the museum — it couldn't go any faster — and the staff cleaned the kegs manually. It was all too slow. An automated keg-washing and filling system was needed. Bang, there's a hundred grand. Emerson's didn't have $100,000 lying around, so for the first time in a while they needed to borrow. Their long-term bank, National, would only lend the money if they got personal guarantees from each director. Some of the directors were shareholders, but one was independent and unwilling to give a personal guarantee to the loan because he didn't have any skin in the game. The brewery changed banks and ASB found a way to lend the money by taking general security over plant.

Creating capacity happened incrementally until it needed to happen exponentially. More tanks could be added, more kegs could be filled, more staff could be employed, but eventually 14 Wickliffe Street ran out of room. The brewery needed big investment — the brewery either had to move again or try something new.

Other things biting included logistics and the cost of freight. As the North Island market grew and more beer headed across Cook Strait, the margins diminished. Having more demand further afield actually cost the business money.

Building another brewery in the North Island became an option, but the directors had seen the hoops they needed to jump through to borrow just $100,000. The bank wouldn't loan them the millions they needed for a new brewery.

They couldn't go to the shareholders and ask for another injection of funds. They'd only recently started getting a dividend beyond a free box of beer. Besides, most of the shareholders had been on board for over 20 years and had already given a cash injection of $400,000 on top of their original $93,000. The bulk of them had retired, some had died, and most had entered a period in their lives where consuming their wealth rather than growing it was the order of the day. Ingrid Emerson, the majority shareholder, was in her seventies. She had nothing left to give and nor did the others.

Private equity wouldn't work as it would dilute the investment of the original shareholders and take control of the brewery away from what was still effectively the Emerson's family.

Contract brewing — where another brewery produces the beer on your behalf — landed on the table as an option. Many New Zealand breweries operate this way — and Richard knew how the model worked as Yeastie Boys from Wellington had started brewing their beer under contract at Invercargill Brewery.

Contract brewing didn't interest Richard, however. He noted it could be difficult to reproduce flavour at another location due to water composition, how the raw materials interacted with the water, brewing methodology of the host brewery — the 'terroir' as he called it. The board minutes recorded as much, saying: 'The flavour of Emerson's beers are VERY important to Richard and the brand . . . History suggests flavour will change' if the beers were brewed under contract.

The brewery had become a giant trapped in a cage of its own making. With nowhere to turn and no move that made sense, Richard felt constrained. Recently married, into his late forties and with a house he wanted to renovate in Middlemarch, he felt he'd reached a point in his life where he should have been enjoying the fruits of his 20-year slog.

After twenty years of not having anything and not being able to do much else, I felt constrained by the business, by the work and the travel. I had no money, nothing. I really had nothing. Without an exit strategy I was a prisoner of the business and that's not what I wanted. I wanted to be someone who helped the business in a constructive way, but also had something in my back pocket — that was better than working my butt off for nothing and not being able to do anything else.

The first approach that would unlock the giant from its cage came in August 2011 at Wellington's annual Beervana festival.

Danny Phillips, head of marketing at Lion, and operations manager Simon Taylor, now the general manager of microbreweries for Lion, arranged to meet Richard and Norma at Lion's Wellington headquarters — what used to be the Mac's brewery on the waterfront.

Phillips said it was a case of Lion 'putting a toe in the water' after a lot of internal assessment about the state of craft beer as a growing market.

Lion were courting other breweries at the same time. It's common knowledge they flirted with Tuatara and scouted a couple of other prominent breweries as well. Lion didn't know exactly what they were looking for, but once they'd eyeballed Richard they had a better idea.

'This was just us putting to Richard, on one piece of paper, an offer to take a small stake in Emerson's, say 40 per cent, or a distribution deal, or even a 51 per cent stake,' Phillips said. 'We didn't have full takeover in mind — we just wanted a relationship with them. Richard wasn't hugely surprised because they'd had approaches before.'

Unlike previous deals presented to Emerson's — with large corporates turning up with teams of lawyers — Lion's process came with just a handful of key people. But it remained a long, slow dance involving two organisations warily circling each other, checking each other out, treading carefully.

'It did take quite a long time, 14 to 15 months from memory, but we didn't want to force the issue — we wanted to do the right thing by Richard, the Emerson's crew, the shareholders — and it was genuinely about a partnership not a takeover,' Phillips said.

***

HE BELIEVED HE HAD TO EXTRICATE HIMSELF FROM THE BREWERY NOW OR CONTINUE TO BE TRAPPED THERE UNTIL HE DIED AND THEN HAVE IT SOLD AFTER HE WAS GONE. LION PRESENTED A THIRD WAY — TO CASH UP HIS SHARE AND CONTINUE TO WORK AT THE BREWERY. RICHARD FELT HE HELD A WINNING HAND. DITTO LION.

***

Lion understood Emerson's had a kind of magic they couldn't reproduce — if they could have, they would have — and that gave the Dunedin company an upper hand. 'We knew that if we didn't protect the magic, we'd be wasting our money — and we'd be accused of corporatising it or homogenising it. We wanted the richness and depth of the Emerson's story — the reason people were attracted to the beers and brand.'

The questions from Lion included: Do you want to work with us? How do you see it happening?

Emerson's came back with: What would happen to our people? What would the beers look like? Who would control the recipes? Would it be a separate legal entity?

'You can't condense that stuff into one catch-up,' Phillips said. 'It was the first time we'd done this since buying Mac's — and it was a lot different to Mac's. We were figuring it out as we went along. Lots of questions popped up, lots of ideas popped up, there was lots of "We'll think about that. What do you think of this?"'

For the best part of a year, a handful of Lion representatives would — in Phillips' words — 'sneak down to Dunedin' to meet Richard and other directors in 'secret' at the office of Emerson's accountants, WHK.

The initial 40 per cent offer gradually morphed into a question from Emerson's that shocked the team at Lion: What does a full takeover look like?

Richard recognised an opportunity to finally reward his loyal shareholders — especially his mother — for their 20 years of support. And — in what Norma would call the paradox of his generosity and self-focus — he saw a clear opportunity for himself. He believed he had to extricate himself from the brewery now or continue to be trapped there until he died and then have it sold after he was gone. Lion presented a third way — to cash up his share and continue to work at the brewery. Richard felt he held a winning hand. Ditto Lion.

Lion's attitude was if they bought the whole thing they bought me too. I was part of the deal. What I discovered from Lion through the process is that they had looked at other breweries — a few — but it came down to me being a personality and a tangible part of the brand. That was a factor that took them down the path of negotiating with me. They had given me several options — distribution, partial buyout — but full buyout was the only option for me.

First, I was thinking of the shareholders, and second, sometimes you have to be a bit selfish and create your own exit plan at the same time. A total buyout was the best way forward — I would have something in the back pocket as well as rewarding the shareholders.

Some of the shareholders had their own concerns and the most common one was: Will you be okay, Richard? Will you be happy? I was surprised to hear that, but it was also great to hear that concern.

I had nothing at the beginning and, at one point, the shareholders realised I was overworked and underpaid and they decided to forgo their own dividends to create some shares for me. I then bought more shares in the capital raise, but that left me heavily in debt. With a total buyout, I could make up for the past. It had to be all or nothing. Everyone was looking at me and I had to make that final call — but it was a no-brainer.

The necessity of ongoing secrecy around the drawn-out negotiations threatened to derail two of Richard's longest friendships.

During the protracted negotiations, Rob Smillie decided to sell his shares to free up cash. Richard couldn't tell him to sit tight, that a potentially big pay day was around the corner, as he'd signed a confidentiality agreement. Richard had to bite his tongue, saying nothing as Rob cashed out. Richard bought his shares.

'The main reason I invested was to say, "Let's give this a crack and see what comes of it,"' Smillie said. 'It seemed like a good idea — we knew it was a quality product and people enjoyed it. Dad would go down and help out at the bottling plant — he was interested in the whole thing. It was fascinating to see it grow and turn into a professional operation. We never got any dividends, but it didn't matter, a mixed dozen every Christmas was enough. But the time came when I needed to release some cash and I knew Richard wanted some more shares.'

The brewery's accountants worked out a share value and Smillie sold his stake to Richard for about $35,000. 'I was happy with that at the time but . . . when they sold to Lion I went back and asked, "Do you think that was a fair price?"'

He calculated that under the Lion deal, his payout would have been three or four times higher. It put a cool edge on their relationship for some time, and Richard wished it could have been different, but equally realised he had no choice but to stay quiet. Besides, the valuation done at the time had been calculated quite differently to the formula Lion would later use. When Smillie exited his shareholding, the brewery had to factor in a future capital expenditure just to keep up with demand. The constraints it faced in terms of future investment pushed down the share value.

Even closer to the sale, the internal assessment of the brewery's value didn't come close to Lion's offer. In August 2012, Emerson's accountants had done their own valuation and landed on approximately $3.5 million

— less than half what Lion would eventually offer. There were a number of reasons for this, not the least being the company would have been forced to borrow or do another capital raise to build a new brewery.

The accountants noted the lack of control of distribution, the reliance on Richard as 'The Brand', that the shares were not really 'liquid' as they were not readily saleable, and growth in the industry had brought in more competitors, dubbed a 'competitive nuisance'. That assessment valued the shares at $9.61 each. Still, that drama between Richard and Rob would not play out until after the sale was announced.

In August 2012, a more immediate problem presented itself. With the paperwork close to being signed, an announcement was still some months away as Lion and the Emerson's board gave themselves plenty of lead time to get their respective houses in order and to inform everyone who needed to know ahead of the inevitable headlines.

The secrecy of the process left many people in the dark, including Chris O'Leary. While Richard's closest friend, Chris wasn't a shareholder or a director. He was an employee. And a disgruntled one.

'For months on end, I couldn't get a decision about anything. I was being stymied. I couldn't buy new tanks, I couldn't bring on new staff. I was incredibly frustrated,' O'Leary said.

The tipping point came just before the sale. The London Olympics loomed and an influential athlete on the New Zealand team approached O'Leary with a too-good-to-be-true proposal.

Eric Murray, part of the unbeatable New Zealand rowing pair alongside Hamish Bond, loved Emerson's beer. The Olympic team had Moa as a beer sponsor. The athletes were obliged to drink Moa inside New Zealand House and at the Olympic village, but outside that environment, they could drink whatever they wanted.

Murray approached O'Leary and said the team would prefer to drink Emerson's Pilsner. He said his sponsors would pay for everything — and could he get a pallet shipped to a hotel in London, where they'd hide it so Moa wouldn't know about it.

'Fantastic,' O'Leary thought, 'what a brilliant guerrilla marketing campaign.'

He practically ran to Bob and Richard, but hit a brick wall when they said no. He couldn't believe his ears — all they had to do was put the Pilsner on a pallet and someone else would not only pay for the beer,

BIRD DOG

Richard has made a number of beers that reference the Dunedin scene, including Tally-Ho (after a song by The Clean) and North by North West (The Bats), but only one has become a permanent part of the Emerson's line-up: Bird Dog.

The name references an album by The Verlaines, which features a song of the same name. The song contains the line: 'I love this imported German beer/They know how to make it over there.' Bird Dog, the beer, however, is nothing like a traditional German lager but is an American-style India Pale Ale. There are huge hop chords of ripe stonefruit on nose, a bassline of juicy malt, and pithy backbeat as the hops assert themselves at the end of a super-long finish.

they'd pay for it to be shipped to London to be consumed by a captive audience. What's not to love?

'No,' came the reply.

'This was on top of a whole lot of other decisions I needed to have made, but even the marketing and business plans were on hold. I told Bob, "That's it. I'm out of here. I'm taking a few days to think about things."'

O'Leary walked out, hired a car, drove up through the Lewis Pass, playing the Black Keys on the stereo, and landed at Mapua near Nelson. There he brewed beer with Jim Matranga, who ran the Golden Bear Brewery.

'I got my soul back,' O'Leary said. 'So, I headed back to Emerson's and told myself if these guys haven't got their act together, I'll move on and do something else.'

He got back to be asked to attend a meeting at the accountant's office. 'I'd said some pretty rough things before I left and then I just disappeared, so I said to my wife, Aggie, "I think this is it." She said, "Don't worry, I've got my job, we'll get through."'

In the boardroom, the directors handed O'Leary a confidentiality agreement to sign.

'Can you tell me more?' he asked. 'No, not until you sign,' they said.

'I made sure it was a confidentiality agreement before I signed it. And they said: "Right, now we can talk. As of next month, Emerson's will be owned by Lion, they'll be the sole shareholder."'

'My first reaction — and comment — was, "What the fuck have you done?" We had no debt, only a handful of shareholders, we could have raised more money, gone to the bank. We had a business that was going so well — why a complete sell-out now? What had gone wrong? This business doesn't need this, what's happening?

'Then I thought: shit, I don't have a job.'

Assured that he did in fact have a job; that he would get a handsome bonus if he stayed on for at least 18 months after the sale; that all the other staff would stay; and that all brewing would remain in Dunedin, O'Leary started to calm down.

'Ingrid was one of the key drivers of all that — as majority shareholder, she demanded all that and she demanded that me, Bob and Richard be kept on.'

Once he'd taken a few deep breaths, O'Leary started to see the logic — the age of the shareholders, the fact they had no more cash to give, that their kids were asking 'where's the return on this bloody investment?'. On top of that, he knew as well as anyone that the brewery had 'the wobbles' in terms of capacity.

'Richard had never imagined the New Zealand public would buy more than a million litres of Emerson's beer — the brewery at Wickliffe Street had been designed with that as capacity. Richard had thought that at a million litres he could just cap it and cruise — that it was within his capability as a person, as a manager. He felt he could deal with that. That was 20,000 litres a week — four brews of 5000 litres. He never thought they'd get beyond that or need to — it wasn't deemed possible that any more than that could be sold.

'But that's where things were — we were coming to a screaming halt because there was no other capacity left.'

O'Leary also realised Richard had been 'under a non-stop, relentless hammer' for over 20 years and if anyone deserved to enjoy the payoff for that hard work then it was Richard.

. . .

In closing the deal, the Emerson's directors stood unified in their belief that only a total buyout could work. As Phillips recalled, 'It evolved to the point when they said, "Can you put the offer down on paper?"'

The directors then presented the deal to the shareholders and, in that regard, their question didn't concern money — with Lion paying $21.77 per share, the return was substantial — rather the worry became what would happen to Richard. 'As the discussion moved in that direction, it started to become obvious that the shareholders would get a healthy return for their support of Richard, and that Richard and team would get to do what they loved without worrying about capex and cash flow . . . for Richard to keep doing what he loved became the more attractive proposition for them.

'Richard's ultimate goal from the start was to share good beer with more people. He got there in a roundabout way. Never in any of those discussions was the focus on money — the accountants looked after that — it was important, but it wasn't the focus. It was about protecting the beers, protecting the people, protecting the authenticity and the integrity, and about what Richard's role would be. It was all about that rather than the money.'

Ingrid drove a lot of the deal-making towards the end. Phillips admitted it felt like 'she was testing us towards the end to see if we were as legit as we were coming across.

'Ingrid liked to see the whites of your eyes. She wasn't heavily involved in the background during the early discussions, but near the end she was right there telling us that these people — Richard, Chris, Bob and others — were really important and we need assurances around them, around Richard, and that this was to stay a Dunedin-centric brand and we were, "Yep, we totally agree with all that."'

When Ingrid, Richard and the board presented the deal to the other shareholders, the information included how much they would get and that the agreement entailed buying all the shares. If anyone didn't want to sell, Lion would come back with another proposal. To assuage any doubters, Ingrid wrote to them:

> *To friends and shareholders,*
> *You all gave us the opportunity to start Richard in his small venture*
> *20 years ago. After a slow start he developed very distinctive beers*
> *and his market increased. You were all very patient!*
> *This offer has been developing over a lengthy time and does give us*
> *ageing shareholders a wonderful exit strategy.*
> *Richard and I feel comfortable with this offer and all it entails.*
> *Ingrid Emerson*

Everyone agreed to sell. For the Lion team, getting Ingrid's seal of approval on the deal proved critical. 'If Ingrid felt like we'd done right by Emerson's and Richard — she's the person I would take most seriously as an arbiter,' Phillips said. 'We inked the deal and then gave ourselves a number of months to prepare for the market announcement, making sure we got to staff and stakeholders first. It was about Richard being able to communicate to those people, which because of his deafness made it a slightly longer process than it might have been.'

Signing off on the deal was a relief. I was really happy for the shareholders that I could give something back. But they were more worried about me, asking would

PEOPLE LOVED EMERSON'S AS THE
ANTITHESIS OF THE 'BIG BOYS' —
A SMALL REGIONAL BREWERY AT
THE BOTTOM OF NEW ZEALAND,
LED BY A COLOURFUL CHARACTER
WHO MADE UNUSUALLY TASTY
BEERS AND WHO HAD BATTLED
THE ODDS TO SUCCEED. TO MANY
OF THOSE FANS, WHO THOUGHT
THEY KNEW AND UNDERSTOOD
EMERSON'S AND RICHARD, SELLING
OUT OR CHANGING SIDES WAS
INCONCEIVABLE.

Richard be okay. But I said as long as the shareholders are happy then I'm okay.
It was difficult to let go of my baby, but I kept telling myself that one day I was
going to need an exit strategy. I'll never walk away from my child — I will always
be connected to it. There will always be something that keeps me involved in the
business, even if it's not making beer.
— Ingrid

Next, Richard had to prepare for the announcement — to the staff and to
the public. He knew being the first brewery to sell to a multinational in this
new era of 'craft' would cause a lot of noise.

In 2000, when Lion bought Mac's from the McCashin family, the beer
revolution hadn't begun. That sale slipped through without a ripple. Now
Emerson's had legions of fans who felt they had a stake in a flagship brewery
leading the charge for good beer. People loved Emerson's as the antithesis
of the 'big boys' — a small regional brewery at the bottom of New Zealand,
led by a colourful character who made unusually tasty beers and who had

battled the odds to succeed. To many of those fans, who thought they knew and understood Emerson's and Richard, selling out or changing sides was inconceivable.

Richard braced for a reaction — but first he had to tell his staff.

The sale of Emerson's to Lion lifted a load off Richard's shoulders. Photo by Jed Soane, The Beer Project.

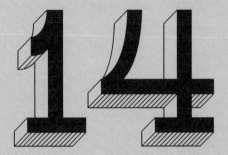

THE
AFTERMATH

Back before the sale went through, I was a little nervous about the concept of selling out. What would the punters think? Would they continue to buy our product? Would my shareholders be happy? All those thoughts ran through my mind. But the shareholders were more than happy to see a healthy return on their investment, and concerns from the public that Emerson's would become a 'watered-down mass-produced product' were quickly allayed. The small amount of negative feedback proved to be just knee-jerk reactions and they were quickly forgotten.

Emerson's Taieri George is released every year on George Emerson's birthday: 6 March.

There were just too many positive vibes going around. I was also worried about what people in the industry would think of me. One brewer came up to me and said, 'Richard, you have given us hope.' What I did and what I went through opened the door for others.

'I cried,' said Emerson's brewing team leader Jim Falconer when he heard the sale news at a staff meeting on Monday, 5 November 2012. Like the rest of the staff, he had no idea about the sale until he heard the announcement from Richard that morning.

The business had just hired a young brewer, Sam White, and when everyone was called to the Monday-morning meeting, Falconer figured they'd be welcoming Sam to Emerson's. 'Instead, it was, "We've sold to Lion." I was horrified. I felt betrayed.'

For Falconer, and others, it felt like the end of something important. 'The dream was over. At that stage we felt we were on a crusade — and when you're on a crusade it helps if you have something you're the opposite of. We thought we were part of the craft crusade against blandness and mindlessness. It was probably a bad mindset to be in, but that's how we felt. Lion were the people we'd been fighting against — they were the opposite of what we were about — and now we'd been absorbed by them. Ideologically, it felt like it couldn't work.'

While the reaction from within Emerson's stayed contained within 14 Wickliffe Street — when the sale became public knowledge the next day, the howls of outrage made themselves heard over the other news of the day — the Melbourne Cup and the US presidential election. Scheduling a controversial announcement for a busy news day is a great corporate strategy, yet the Emerson's sale cut through all that noise.

On the day after the public announcement of the sale, I was in Central Otago because the plan was that I had to carry on as if nothing had happened. I'll never forget driving back to Dunedin from Queenstown that morning. At one stage I had to pull over to the side of the road to answer a text and I saw a copy of the *Otago Daily Times* sticking out of a letter box and I could see a part of the headline which read: 'Lion buys . . .' I thought, 'Wow, I've made the headlines.'

Bob King said the 'vitriol' aimed at Richard and the brewery started that day and kept going for weeks. Three well-known independent bars —

MUCH OF THE ANGER WAS AROUND EMERSON'S SELLING AS MUCH AS IT WAS ABOUT LION PUTTING ITS LARGE PAWPRINT ON WHAT HAD BEEN AN ICONIC INDEPENDENT BREWERY — THE FEAR WAS THAT THE BEER WOULD BE DUMBED DOWN, ACCOUNTANTS WOULD CALL THE SHOTS, AND THE BREWERY WOULD LOSE ITS SOUL. OUTRAGED PUNTERS ACCUSED RICHARD OF BEING A SELL-OUT — OF ABANDONING THEM AND HIS PRINCIPLES.

Wellington's Hashigo Zake, The Free House in Nelson and Christchurch's Cassels Brewery — all announced boycotts of Emerson's. Punters took to Facebook vowing never to drink the beer again.

Much of the anger was around Emerson's selling as much as it was about Lion putting its large pawprint on what had been an iconic independent brewery — the fear was that the beer would be dumbed down, accountants would call the shots, and the brewery would lose its soul. Outraged punters accused Richard of being a sell-out — of abandoning them and his principles.

To understand the reaction, you have to understand the journey beer had taken from 'micro' — kind of cute and different, but not necessarily substantial — to 'craft' which, as Falconer noted, felt like a crusade. From roughly 2007 through to 2012, what had been an alternative — cottage — industry became a movement.

It's not entirely helpful to use broad-brush stereotypes — but the beer scene stopped being the domain of roman sandal-wearing beardy blokes

who home-brewed. It became a bit more cool, urban, underground —
and political. It became counter-revolutionary, a subculture with roots in
flavour, but with aspirations for change. It pitted small and independent
against big and corporate, put handcrafted up against industrial.

Craft brewers stood for the opposite of corporate breweries — faces
versus faceless. A beer lover could go to a festival and meet the person who
made the beer, have a conversation about it. Personal connection mattered.
It was us (who drank flavoursome beer made by a person we could see) and
them (the invisible, foreign-owned corporates who made mass swill). Craft
pitted small-scale against factory. Craft played an honesty card — devoid of
marketing and spin. Craft gave fans a sense of ownership — a stake in the
revolution. Every pint or 500ml bottle of craft beer chipped another brick
from the crumbling wall of corporate beer. Admittedly, this period of true
revolution was relatively short-lived because it didn't take long for craft to
jump from anti-establishment to conventional. A bandwagon came around
the corner and filled up fast.

Emerson's sale was a signal that the craft-beer train had switched
tracks. It flagged a change in the fight — the big guys had lobbed a grenade,
disrupting the disrupters. Here was a bubble-bursting eye-opener that
making great beer was not just a noble calling — it was also a business, a
big-money business. And people who had been part of the revolution, who'd
helped create that us-and-them mentality, felt one of the strongest fighters
had crossed over to become one of them. It felt like treason.

'The vitriol aimed at Richard after the sale was horrific,' Bob King
recalled. 'For many he was suddenly the Antichrist. Because of their
personal association, they felt betrayed. We had people come to the shop to
tell us they'd never buy the brand again. That stuff hurt Richard, he felt it
because it was his brewery. But the fans felt they also had an ownership of
it — their reaction was, "How dare you sell this brewery that I feel I own?"
Nothing changed with the beer but the brand connect was broken.'

Richard Emerson's relentlessly positive, go-forward attitude is the
kind of trait possessed by so many successful business people. Yes, he had
moments early when he wanted to chuck it all away but after decompressing
he picked himself up and went to work the next morning at 6am to plough
through another 12-hour day, putting yesterday's drama behind him and
starting afresh with a new batch of beer.

Yes, he butted heads with his father for 10 years over spending money on what Richard saw as necessities and what George regarded as nice-to-haves. And after each 'no' Richard went out and found another way to make things work. From childhood he's had an unrelenting positivity and an explorer's attitude of looking ahead rather than behind.

That's not to say he wouldn't get angry, frustrated or tearful — but moving on has been the default setting. It was an attitude that allowed him to give Rob Smillie a black eye for taunting him and yet they ended up being best friends. He bought one disastrous Mini and when he wrote it off he bought another one — having learned what to look out for. If things broke, like bike axles or grain mills — he didn't wallow in misfortune but found a way to fix the problem.

IT'S NOT IN RICHARD'S NATURE TO PITCH A TENT AT CAMP NEGATIVITY — HE'LL JUMP ON HIS BIKE AND RIDE ON, LITERALLY DEAF TO THE CRITICS AND NAYSAYERS.

It's not in Richard's nature to pitch a tent at Camp Negativity — he'll jump on his bike and ride on, literally deaf to the critics and naysayers.

He treated those searing criticisms the same way, brushing them aside and focusing on the future. His antidote to the venom was his innate positivity. 'The small amount of negative feedback proved to be just knee-jerk reactions and they were quickly forgotten. There were just too many positive vibes going around.'

. . .

Richard weathered the storm of disapproval in a fashion matched only by Lion's faith in their newly acquired business. The purchase could have backfired given a strong enough mutiny, but Lion had faith in Richard's personality. They'd done their research and believed in him.

Lion chose to buy Emerson's instead of other contenders for a bunch of

reasons. The place mattered — rooted in Dunedin — both in the sense of a physical home and a local tribe of devoted consumers. The brewery had its own recipes and creative processes ensuring unique and novel beers. The brewery could run independently of head office, as a quantum package it could chug along under its own steam with Lion providing external support when needed. And finally, Lion bought the brewery because of Richard. Plenty of other breweries had similar qualities to Emerson's — connected to a place, with their own recipes and independent — but none of them had the depth of connection between brewer and brand that Emerson's possessed. A deep connection between Richard and his brand created an X factor that was impossible to ignore.

The marketing team at Lion like to use the 12 personality archetypes developed by psychologist Carl Jung — if a brand can be captured by one or two of Jung's archetypes then it's a strong brand easily articulated in-house.

A few years after buying Emerson's, for instance, Lion made a stunning decision to buy Panhead Custom Ales out of Upper Hutt. The blue-collar, petrol-head, irreverent brand was only three years old when Lion swooped — and the overriding reason was brand power. The brand captured precisely, by Jung's archetype, the rebel, a personality with outrageously big ideas who inspires others to join them.

Lion's consumer research prior to buying Emerson's revealed a primary and secondary archetype that nailed down Richard and his brewery — the sage and the jester. They come together as the sage jester.

The sage is about truth, wisdom and sharing knowledge — the sage is a master in his or her field, but open, approachable and generous. As an industry leader, renowned for brewing to style and delivering quality, the sage archetype fitted Emerson's like a beloved tee-shirt. Richard too, as the master, respected far and wide for his skill, knowledge, impeccable palate and willingness to share, is a sage in his own right. The jester is Richard's wry humour, which in turn permeates the brand. He's cheeky, irreverent, effervescent and not afraid to make fun of himself or take a joke which makes him easy to relate to.

As Lion's marketing head Danny Phillips noted: 'The brand could have been earnest and classical, closed-off and a bit wankerish, but Richard's approachability, the way he was able to talk to anyone, to create instant

Chris O'Leary has thoroughly embraced Dunedin's Scottish heritage.

rapport through making a joke or his self-deprecating humour allows people to approach him without worrying about his deafness, and that allows them to approach the brand as well. He literally grew his brand by talking to people at beer events — it's his passion.'

Capturing the brand so easily speaks to its authenticity — the soul of Emerson's since day one. 'Richard's heart is what shone through,' Phillips said. 'People wanted to talk about him because he's so special.'

The connection people made with Richard in turn made Emerson's the front-runner for Lion. 'We started with three breweries we were looking at, but it soon became obvious Emerson's were the clear winner. The brand was just so deep.'

Lion's takeover was the first bold move under new managing director Rory Glass, who emphasised his belief in Emerson's as 'highly credible, authentic and with some passionate guys behind it'.

The authenticity would become a façade, however, if Richard, Chris O'Leary and other key personnel such as Bob King, didn't stay on. As part of the sale process, Lion guaranteed that trio a retention bonus split between them if they were to stay on for three years post-sale.

Despite his concerns, even brewing team-leader Jim Falconer stayed on. 'It seems to have worked and I've got a bit more faith now, it's taken a long time to see that their intentions were good. And they also have faith in what we're doing — that we're profitable and can make good beer. They're quite hands off, which is different to what I'd thought it would be.'

That hands-off approach helped punters believe that Emerson's, if not independently owned, at least operated that way. It's no secret that Lion has invested heavily in the brewery — but it's been an investment in things that make better beer: equipment and people — not marketing.

· · ·

Richard Emerson is so well-loved, so universally respected, that no one within the tight-knit beer community begrudged him his financial windfall. The sale made him an overnight millionaire — just — but many believed that undervalued what Richard has done for the brewing industry as a whole.

'Richard completely and wholeheartedly has a passion and soul for flavour, taste and beer — he's built that business organically and it's all come from within,' said Chris O'Leary. 'He was never driven by a dollar. Yes, he got

$1 million out of the deal but he probably deserved more. He doesn't have to work now, doesn't have to be at the brewery, but he loves being around people, loves the beer, loves the food, loves the energy around it, loves what he's created.'

Pete Gillespie, brewer and founder at Garage Project, one of New Zealand's most admired breweries, so adored Emerson's beer he once applied for a job there. 'Richard's such a fucking legend, such an icon. Way back before I had ever worked in a brewery anywhere — back when I was home-brewing — I wrote a letter to Emerson's asking for a job there. I just loved what they were doing with beer. They were immensely inspirational. When they sold they copped a lot of shit, but it was time for investors to get something out because anyone who owns a brewery knows very little ever comes out.'

RICHARD EMERSON IS SO WELL-LOVED, SO UNIVERSALLY RESPECTED, THAT NO ONE WITHIN THE TIGHT-KNIT BEER COMMUNITY BEGRUDGED HIM HIS FINANCIAL WINDFALL.

As Emerson's negotiated with Lion, Garage Project started out on their own journey. Gillespie, his brother, Ian, and co-founder Jos Ruffell set up shop in an old garage in Wellington's Aro Valley. They had a 50-litre brewery — nothing more than a home-brew-sized operation smaller than what Richard had brewed in his garage at Ravensbourne. Garage Project's nanobrewery sat on the freshly painted floor of the large garage with the only other object in the room being a huge couch Ruffell had bought so they had somewhere to sit.

'The garage, from outside, looked totally derelict. We'd tidied up the inside a little bit, painted the floor . . . We were there doing our thing one day when Richard suddenly popped in. He'd snooped around and found us and came to visit. He was so supportive, so lovely, but he was almost pissing himself with laughter at the fact our couch was bigger than our brewery.

That captured the real enthusiasm he has for life — an almost childlike, unrestrained enthusiasm.'

A few years later, Gillespie went to a beer festival in Christchurch and stayed at the famous Pomeroy's Pub. 'I was lying in bed, but couldn't get to sleep because there was a really noisy bathroom fan going in the next room. It might have had a loose bearing or something because the sound was awful. I was thinking, "Who can sleep with this bathroom fan going like that? They're going to have to switch it off soon, surely." But it went all night and I had the worst sleep. In the morning, I was in the hall when Richard walked out of the room next door — and I thought, "There we go, that explains it!"

'The thing is he hasn't let his deafness become a disability in the slightest — his passion for brewing has just totally overwhelmed any disability. It sounds patronising to say it's brave, but he's just so public, he's just out there. He's a delight in large groups of people. He has my deepest respect on all levels.'

Stu McKinlay of Yeastie Boys voiced a pro-Lion, pro-Richard argument

Richard with Lion's managing director Rory Glass at the opening of the Emerson's brewery and restaurant in 2016. Photo by Michael Donaldson.

at the time of the sale. He regarded Richard as a mentor, friend and inspiration, and shared Richard's delight at the brewery sale. 'Richard didn't set out to become a millionaire — he set out to make beautiful beers that changed people's lives. And he changed my life. I can still remember the moment I discovered this beer with a weird name, Bookbinder, which came out before any other beers had word names. The funny name drew my attention and it blew my mind with the New Zealand hop flavour. I had been trying beer from New Zealand microbreweries for years so I wasn't new to this, but that was well ahead of its time.

'Richard was just next level. Without a doubt he was the inspiration for everyone in the next wave of brewing — 8 Wired, Panhead, Liberty — they were all heavily inspired by what Emerson's did on the beer front. He inspired me — we've received so much help from him, and that's influenced me in terms of how much I like to help others.

'I always call him The Godfather — he wasn't the first but he was the most important. I would definitely put him ahead of the others regarded as leaders in the industry . . . people fall in love with his enthusiasm for beer and flavour. He's a friend and hero.'

Kelly Ryan, a food science student under JP Dufour at Otago and now one of the most admired brewers in the country for the work he does at Wellington's Fork & Brewer, had his beer journey shunted onto a different track by Bookbinder. 'That was a revelation with its mystical, soft, gentle, low carbonation. Richard always understood balance — there are not many of his beers that you drink where one's enough.'

Ryan, who has collaborated on a version of Emerson's JP, believed Richard's obstinate determination allowed him to survive the 25-year journey from scrabbling start-up to multi-million-dollar business, and that determination has dragged the entire New Zealand industry with it.

'Stubbornness and sheer bloody-mindedness have got him and the New Zealand brewing industry to where we are now — that's where revolutions begin, with bloody-mindedness.'

And Richard's obstinate fighting qualities are critical to thriving in the Lion's den. 'The cool thing is that they are now part of a global brewery, but they haven't changed a bit — that's a lot to do with the stubbornness of Richard and Chris. To get bought out and become more experimental is the opposite of every other buyout in the world.'

Ryan admires Richard's ability to find a way to share his passion with

the world despite his deafness. 'He's such a great communicator, I don't notice at all that he's deaf any more because he's so good at getting his point across — like his early beers, he has no filter. He is inspirational for me. As someone who learned the trade overseas, it still blows my mind what he achieved here. He is a craft pioneer and there are many things we wouldn't have here if it wasn't for Richard.'

Hello Grandma . . .
I still want to run a brewpub one day as a family enterprise with a restaurant. But I'll have to look into it very carefully. I want to keep it small and manageable as well as being within financial grasp.

That postcard Richard sent to his grandmother from Perth in 1990 now sits framed on the wall of the entrance to the fourth and final Emerson's Brewery at 70 Anzac Avenue, Dunedin. The brewery sits alongside the same railway line that carries tourists on the Taieri Gorge Railway. Just behind the brewery stands a railway overbridge where George Emerson frequently photographed trains.

For the first time in his business life, Richard didn't have to fret over the move, with Lion handling all the logistics.

Moving a brewery, with sales still climbing, is never an easy task. Looking back, the move from 4 to 9 Grange Street was the easiest one of them all. The 9 Grange Street to 14 Wickliffe Street was the hardest one, months of sleepless nights thinking about the move, the three months of seven-days-a-week brewing to fill the tanks at Wickliffe Street, one brew per day onto the beer truck with the 1200-litre tank strapped down.

I'm proud to say the first three fermenters from 4 Grange Street are still with us on the new site and still being used to produce special brews. Some new gear and hand-me-downs from Lion really ramped up the potential of the brewery.

While the building was constructed almost two years after planning, the market had changed quite significantly. We could not have predicted the market shift to 330ml bottles as a result of the new lowered blood-alcohol limit. The good thing was that our new bottle-filling line was capable of filling different bottle sizes.

Lion's investment in Emerson's has allowed the brewery to continue growing to meet an ever-increasing demand.

Spirits were high when the new brewery was finally launched, 21 June 2016 – complete with Richard's mobile festival bar, aka the 'mini-bar'.

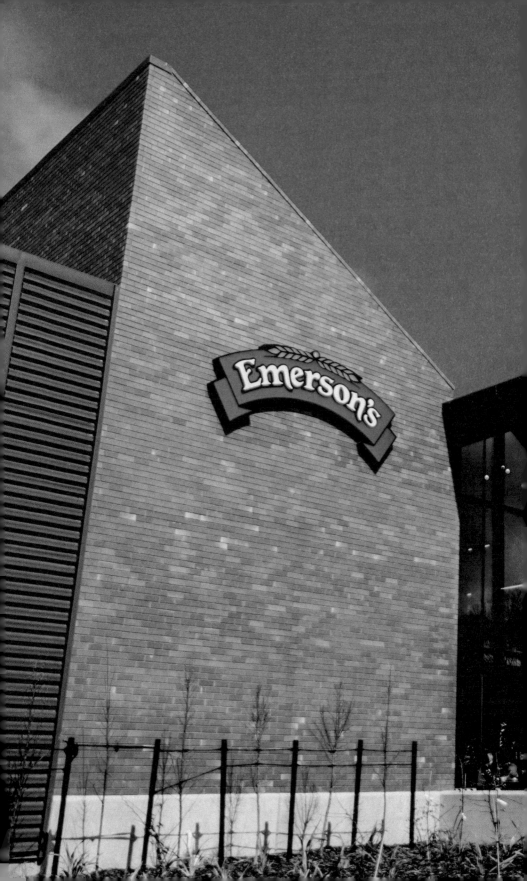

Not long after settling into the new site, the keg cleaner and filler from Wickliffe Street was starting to show strain from being maxed out every working day. Lion gracefully stepped in with a second-hand semi-automatic keg-cleaning and filler line. This has helped us immensely and the old keg filler has gone to Panhead Custom Ales — another hand-me-down or as the accountants say 'a transfer of assets'.

The best thing that's happened recently is the commission of the new Palmer canning line from the USA. The staff are amazed how much quieter it is in operation compared to the bottling line. Most of the output is going to Air New Zealand for their domestic and international flights. I love the sound of a can opening, since I can't really hear a bottle opening but a can I can! 'Paarffft . . .' it's like canned music for the deaf!

The new brewery officially opened on 21 June 2016 with a piping in of the haggis, a Robbie Burns poem and a frenetic performance by The Chills. It was very much a Dunedin experience, something The Chills' Martin Phillipps was proud to be part of. 'I think Richard's one of the most inspirational people in this town. He put his foot down and said this was going to be Dunedin's night. It wasn't going to be taken over by corporates from Auckland and I love that side of him.'

The multi-million-dollar brewery is everything Richard wished for when he penned that postcard a lifetime earlier — he describes it as 'a proper spiritual home for the Emerson's brand' — replete with a small experimental brewery, about the size of his first brew kit from 4 Grange Street, which he plays around with from time to time. The boardroom table carries memories of his earlier ventures — made from recycled rimu timber salvaged from 9 Grange Street.

The plaque on the wall at the entrance is typically Richard: 'This establishment was formally declared open on 21st June 2016 by the Hon. Richard's mum, also known as Ingrid Emerson. In keeping with Dunedin tradition, Richard insisted on bagpipes. Fine for him; he didn't have to listen to them.'

Inside there's a painting of Richard dressed as a masked bandit. It comes with something of an in-joke at the brewery — that Richard's

Previous spread: The building of Emerson's new brewery on Anzac Avenue fulfilled Richard's dream of having a brewpub with his name on it.

Right: Richard's humour comes through in the plaque on the wall of the new brewery.

THIS ESTABLISHMENT
WAS FORMALLY DECLARED
OPEN ON 21ST JUNE 2016
BY THE HON. RICHARD'S MUM,
ALSO KNOWN AS INGRID EMERSON.

IN KEEPING WITH DUNEDIN
TRADITION, RICHARD INSISTED
ON BAGPIPES. FINE FOR HIM;
HE DIDN'T HAVE TO LISTEN
TO THEM.

ESTD 1992

favourite phrase these days is, 'It's not my money.'

Richard's love of trains is evoked in the brewery. The floor of the restaurant has a set of symbolic train tracks running across it. The men's toilet plays the sound of a steam train when the toilet's flushed. Outside, there's a steam locomotive whistle that Richard happily toots, not having to put up with the high-pitched squeal it emits. The booths along one wall of the restaurant look like railway carriages, with windows showing a view of the brewery's landscape.

For a brewer who slaved away for little recompense for 20 years, the benefit of Lion's monetary might is a godsend and Richard enjoys the stress-free bliss of not worrying about where the next dollar will come from. That said, he still campaigns for things he believes the brewery needs: his latest being for Lion to build a railway platform next to the brewery so railcars can pick up passengers. The dream is for the Silver Fern railcar to pick up Emerson's punters and serve them a few beers on the glorious seaside trip up the coast to Waitati and back.

'We've built him a giant beer palace, but he still wants more!' said Danny Phillips, laughing. 'He'll probably get it one day because he's so persistent. He's so entrepreneurial and he's always asking, "What next?" He's full of ideas.'

Another in-joke at Emerson's — although Richard is deadly serious — is Richard's oft-stated dream that Lion will ditch their association with Guinness and replace the famous Dublin drop with his London Porter in all the Irish bars up and down the country.

It's so thrilling to have been involved in building the new brewery — it's the icing on the cake to have something I'm proud of to give to Dunedin, courtesy of Lion. The location is great and closer to my other pleasure — trains. And I have the joy of having an authentic steam locomotive whistle to toot on special occasions. The land was a real eyesore and now it's a great showcase for Dunedin, especially in the cruise ship season with trains and buses going past. If we hadn't sold the brewery to Lion, Dunedin wouldn't have got the wonderful brewery that's there.

Richard's relief at shedding the burden of the brewery is palpable. McKinlay calls him the 'happiest man in beer' while Norma Emerson can see the weight lifted from her husband. 'It's better for him now — previously everything that went wrong was his personal problem. When I first met Richard and heard him talking about his brewery, I thought it was a little garage operation, but when I came to Dunedin and discovered it was actually a big business I was blown away. I couldn't believe how many people were working there and that this deaf person was running it. But what struck me was the sense of family.

'The new brewery went beyond the dream he had for himself. The dream was a brewpub. When I met Richard it was never on the cards that his brewery would become so big or be for sale — we thought Wickliffe Street was the biggest it could get.'

Despite the new brewery's size — it is a Dunedin landmark — the sense of family remains for those connected to it. David Stedman, whose own home-brewing disaster inadvertently sparked the epic Emerson's adventure, is in awe of Richard's achievement. 'I think he's a genius. Even though he repeated sixth form, he did better than many of his peers — it was obvious there was a level of intense brain activity going on in a creative way, but also in a very methodical deductive way. He was always precisely focused. He was very clear about what he wanted to do and there was always that decent intellect at work.

'Sometimes you think, "If he wasn't deaf, how amazingly successful could he have been?" Or would he have squandered everything — like the rest of us — because he wouldn't have had to work so hard? Maybe his deafness gave him an edge. He always had to find another way of doing things — to overcome — but he just shone anyway. Richard always had his own thing going on. He had the added bonus of two very bright and supportive parents who were able to see beyond the circumstances of his deafness and chose the pathway for his education based on the result they wanted.'

Rob Smillie, Richard's long-time friend — he of the black eye from their first meeting — believes Dunedin owes the Emersons a lot for the family's contribution to the city through George's vision and determination with the Taieri Gorge Railway and the brewery. 'I always worried that if the brewery got sold, it would be closed or moved. The fact Lion have invested in the city with infrastructure is fantastic; people can see there's value in it for locals.

'I have a friend in Germany and the first time he came here, he said, "I'll meet you at this great beer place in your city — it's called Emerson's . . . Have you heard of it?" I laughed.

'I'm privileged and honoured to be part of the process. Richard's success demonstrated to people that you can overcome anything — any disability — if you have energy, and he always had energy. He was always optimistic, future-looking, imaginative . . . He didn't dwell on the negative, he had a positive adventurous outlook for what was around the corner.'

From the other side of the world, Helen Emerson revels in the fact that her city features a monument to her brother — her family. 'We always had Alison Holst as our famous relative, and recently I saw my cousin Simon Holst post a picture of himself on Facebook drinking a can of Emerson's on an Air New Zealand flight and I thought, "Wow, we've got our Alison!"

'It was Richard's dream to have a brewpub. He had this vision for it and he got it, dammit. He has worked his butt off for years, doing long physical hours when he was the only person running the entire brewery except for Dad coming in at lunchtime to answer a few calls and Mum labelling bottles. He's done it and it's based on the clarity of his vision combined with hard work. It hasn't come easy, but he's had that focus and perseverance that you don't see in many people — but you see it in people who achieve greatness whether they be athletes or musicians or whatever. That diligence that he's applied is why he was successful.

'When I come home and see that brewery at the end of Frederick Street — holy crap — I wish Dad could see that. I'm so proud!

'Dad and Richard did discuss a strategy for selling from the early days. The brewery was always going to be Richard's retirement plan. I'm not sure what would have happened had Dad lived longer — if he had stayed alive and been involved would that have been the best thing for the brewery's growth? He was so conservative. In many ways, it had to be sold to get the expansion it needed. I'm not sure whether Dad could have walked away and left it to other people with a different approach to risk and different business acumen.'

Helen pauses for a moment to reflect on Richard's story and George's unwavering commitment — not to the brewery as such — but to Richard, to his son. To ensure Richard would have what he needed to get through life with the security he needed but was never guaranteed because of his deafness.

'I wonder if George's support was driven in part by feeling guilty that all the family trips were about his interests — including the fateful trip to Christchurch over Labour Weekend in 1963.'

Perhaps. But unlikely. Yes, that trip changed the lives of Ingrid and George Emerson, but for Ingrid it's not a case of whether it changed things for better or worse — and she could happily make an argument for the former. After all, Richard's success is her success. It's a vindication of the hours upon long hours she dedicated to teaching him to lip-read when others questioned why she put so much effort into her son. And it's not the money, nor the fame that came with her son's rock-star status in the brewing industry. Her reward is in his resilience, the undiminished spirit, the very fact of his success against all conceivable odds.

'He had an attitude of mind that he wasn't going to give up,' Ingrid said, though she could well have been talking about herself. 'Richard probably didn't seem normal when he went to primary school, but he blossomed. Nobody knows what Richard and I did in those early years. I've learned a lot from this life. And seeing him succeed has meant it was so worth it.

'What a wonderful life it's been.'

EPILOGUE

I spoke to Richard late one morning at his Middlemarch home. 'Hi Richard, have you got time for another question?'

'Oh, well, I suppose so . . . What is it?'

I beamed with delight. 'Imagine you had a chance to sit down with your dad over a pint at the new brewery: what would you tell him about the last 16 years since he passed away? How would you sum up the journey you've been on?'

'Michael! This is a heavy question man; this is stuff out of the *Twilight Zone*. You're giving me goose bumps thinking about it. Give me a break, mate!' He leaned back on his chair, brushing his hands through his hair and taking a slow, deep breath.

I smiled with amusement. 'Don't worry, Richard, just give yourself a little time. I think it's a pretty cool way to finish off.'

He shrugged his shoulders, scratching the right side of his head. 'All good, I'll catch up with you in a few days then. Cheerio.'

After that conversation with Michael, I sat staring at the computer screen thinking, 'What the fark am I gonna tell him? Best I just get on with it, I suppose.'

At that moment, I noticed some movement and saw the door had swung open a few inches. 'Norma, is that you?'

I stood up to walk towards the door and saw a shadow . . . bloody hell. It looked like George. Same dark green corduroy pants, same Summit shirt. And there it was, his trademark ginger beard. 'What the hell are you doing here?'

'Michael's been asking everyone he can think of about you, so I figured I'd pop down and talk to you myself. It's been a while . . . I hope you've been behaving.'

'Tell me about it — the bugger even spoke to my Marion!'

George looked a bit pissed off. 'What have you done now, Richard?'

'Yeah, there's a bit for you to catch up on, George,' I said, wondering where to start. It's not every day the ghost of your old dad turns up for a yarn.

George looked me straight in the eye and, with his usual frankness, said, 'Start at the beginning, boy.'

'Well, Dad, after you left, I had a bit of a struggle to keep things on track at the brewery.'

'Tell me you didn't go broke, Richard!'

'Always with an eye on the finances, eh, George?' I laughed. 'Things got tough there for a bit, then I tried to have a break and, well, one thing led to another and I ended up breaking things off with Marian . . .' My voice trailed off.

'What happened?' asked George, even though I wasn't sure he really wanted to know.

I continued, 'I think it was for the best. Things hadn't been working out for a while. I think we both knew it was just a matter of time.'

'Right, okay then. Now tell me about the brewery,' said George, happy to change the subject.

'Hang on a second, there's something else I need to tell you first. I got married again. You'd like Norma, she's a South African girl with a South African attitude. I have to warn you though, she is not much of a train fan and there is no way that she is ever going to be a train widow like Mum!'

While George laughed, I had an idea. 'How about I take you to visit the brewery, Dad?'

'Sure. Two questions though. Where are we? And how are we going to get there?'

'Oh yeah, I forgot to mention that we've moved to Middlemarch — nice and close to the railway, eh, Taieri George . . .'

Dad grinned.

'And in answer to your second question, we'll take the truck.'

George sat quietly in the passenger seat, taking in that landscape he loved so much. There were a couple of hawks soaring above Sutton as we passed. I reckon he was probably thinking about the light on the rocks and how much time he'd spent out here waiting for a train to photograph.

Eventually, he snapped out of his dream. 'Are you still in Grange Street, then?'

It had been a while. 'We've moved a couple of times since you had your hands on the purse-strings,' I laughed. 'Although we did spend some money — we got ourselves a nice new bottling plant that could chug out 5000 bottles on hour!'

Dad had always hated spending money, but even he looked impressed with that.

I continued to give him the rundown while keeping an eye on the winding road to Outram.

'We outgrew the place. Remember Mike Hormann, who I went to primary school with? Well, he and Ruth Houghton bought a building in Wickliffe Street, so we could lease it. We had a bloody good party when we moved in there!'

'Right . . .' said George as he pondered his next question. 'So, just how big is this new place, and are you sure you can afford it?'

I grinned. Same old George. 'Oh, you know, it had a million-litre capacity'.

'What?!' George exclaimed.

I explained to him how things had moved forward, the new share structure, growing staff numbers, our new beers and a bit about the Wickliffe Street site.

BIG RIG

Big Rig, an American Pale Ale, is a reference to the Foden steam truck. Ironically the American Pale Ale has only recently been reinstated to the Emerson's line-up after a gap of almost 20 years. Richard has proved time and again that he is always one step ahead of the trends, but with his first APA — around 20 years ago — he was so far ahead of the curve as to be out of sight. His original APA, featuring an American bald eagle on the label, was such a radical hop-driven and bitter beer it struggled for acceptance and was quietly shelved. It was simply too much, too soon for the Kiwi beer drinker. Since then, thanks to brewers like Epic, Panhead, Garage Project and Liberty, American-style hoppy pale ales have surged in popularity.

Dad seemed to be taking it all in, then a worried look came across his face. 'You said you had to move a couple of times. You haven't had to downsize, have you?' As usual, he was worried for my future.

I just smiled to myself and said nothing as I steered the truck over the bridge towards the new Anzac Avenue brewery and taproom. Dad looked a bit confused as I pointed out the big, new red-brick building with our name emblazoned across it.

'George, all those years you were taking photographs from this bridge, did you ever imagine we'd have a brewery right there?'

George went quiet for a few moments. 'I can't say I did, Richard, I can't say I did.'

As I pulled into the brewery carpark, the look of pride on George's face turned to fear. 'How the hell can you afford this?'

'Let's go inside and I'll explain over a beer.'

George and I walked through the large glass doors into the lobby with its high ceiling and large Emerson's banner.

George struggled to take in what he was seeing. He clearly needed a drink.

We sat down at a booth table and got two pints of London Porter. 'This might taste a bit different to last time you had it. I've been working on the recipe a bit.'

George sipped his beer quietly, then said, 'This is good, it's been a bit dry upstairs. You still have the handpumps?'

An Emerson's branded Foden steam truck is used for promotional events around the country, connecting Richard's brewery back to his love of steam trains.

'Not here. This one's been served on nitro gas with a special nozzle. Flash, eh?'
George nodded.

'Some bars around the country still serve on the handpump though.'

'Around the country, eh? There must be a lot of them for you to have built this place!'

I told Dad the short version of how a couple of the big breweries had approached me about deals, but none of them had seemed right until Lion came along. I explained how I'd been working bloody hard and not really getting anywhere, and that they'd made me an offer.

'You sold the brewery to Lion?' I could tell George was wondering if this was a practical joke.

'Yep. The deal was good. They kept the recipes, they kept the beers, they kept the staff and they kept me. They really didn't want anything to change, besides which, the shareholders got a good return on their investment.'

George looked relieved. 'So, you and your mother are well set up then? And Helen too?'

'Yep, all set up, George. We don't have to worry too much about money any more. Lion have been good to us — I'm working on getting them to build a railway platform outside so the railcar can pick up passengers from here. Our own railway station, how good would that be?'

'That's one of your better ideas,' George laughed as he took in his surroundings. His eyes coming to a halt on something he spotted outside. 'Is that a . . . Foden?!'

'Yep! Our very own Foden steam truck — we use it for doing promotions. I even named a beer after it — Big Rig!'

I could tell Dad was impressed.

'And not only that, we have an Ab whistle outside our boiler.'

George looked even more astonished. 'Where did you get that from?'

I smiled. 'It's Bill Cowan's whistle, at least he gets to hear it across the harbour.'

George sat still for a while. 'I'm glad to know you're all doing well. That's all I ever wanted. It's about time I went back then.'

He finished his drink and stood up to leave. I didn't want him to go. There was still so much I wanted to talk to him about. 'Hey Dad, your photos got published in two books and countless magazines, I'm still busy on the negatives . . .'

My voice trailed off, as George turned around with a smile and mouthed the words, 'Thank you,' before disappearing off into the bright afternoon light.

ACKNOWLEDGEMENTS

The first time I met Richard Emerson we made 200 litres of beer, on a small kit at his third brewery – 14 Wickliffe Street. It was for the Beervana festival a few years back when they had a media brew competition; beer writers were paired with brewers to concoct something for a friendly competition. When I was asked who I'd like to brew with I just about shouted: Richard Emerson.

To me, back in 2011, he was a brewing god – and to others, it turns out. I knew he was deaf but I wasn't prepared for how hard it would be to communicate with him in a noisy brewery – and by hard, I mean it was more Richard who suffered, as I asked him to repeat himself time and again. He could read my lips just fine, although he later commented I had a slightly hard-to-read face. But against the backdrop of a working brewery it was me who struggled to understand him; he was endlessly patient with my need to have things repeated. I learned so much about brewing that day. The beer, Hop off the Press, was also pretty cool – but that was all thanks to Richard who took my rudimentary home-brew recipe and made it delicious.

Since then he's always been available to comment on stories of mine and to help with other books I've written. Four years ago, we talked about writing his biography but I was in the middle of another book and had to decline. We agreed to come back to it some time in the future and thank god we did – because it's a story I'm honoured to have written.

Naturally, Richard plays a critical part in his own story but I cannot thank him enough – again, for his patience, but also for the huge amount of legwork he's done around photographs, documents and racking his memory to make sure we got the story told. And thanks to Norma Emerson for keeping her husband on track and offering up so much of her own important story.

There were so many other people without whom this book could not have been written.

Richard's mother Ingrid is at the heart of what is a family story – after all, she's been there from the start and has been Richard's biggest supporter, along with his late father George, through all phases of his life: from learning to lip-read to starting a brewery with family and friends' money.

Helen Emerson, Richard's younger sister, was an incredible font of memories and stories. Her generosity with family history helped elevate this book to something special. Richard's uncle Alastair Emerson also helped me understand more of the family history.

I thank Richard's long-time friends and supporters – particularly David Stedman, Rob Smillie, Grant Hanan, Mike Hormann, Graeme Berry, Ruth Houghton, as well as Marian Rait, Richard's first wife, who trusted me with telling her part of this story.

Fellow beer writer Geoff Griggs offered valuable insights as well as photographs that appear in this book. Geoff was there for the adolescence of New Zealand's craft beer scene and the industry as a whole owes him a debt of gratitude for preaching good beer to a mainstream audience, when New Zealand's breweries could be listed in the time it took to pull a pint.

I'd also like to thank Richard's staff and colleagues at Emerson's – including Greg Menzies, Jim Falconer and CJ – for their support (hang on Father, we're getting to you . . .) and for making me at home in their home.

A number of people at Lion have also been catalysts for the book coming together – both now and in the past – especially Danny Phillips, Sara Tucker, Dave Pearce and Rory Glass.

And to Jeremy Sherlock and his team at Penguin Random House – thank you for believing in the story, backing both myself and Richard to make it happen and delivering the attention it needed.

Finally – and by no means least – there's one person who poured as much of his heart and soul into this project as I did. Chris O'Leary – Richard's best friend, strongest supporter, long-time colleague and all-round beer genius – drove this book to be the best it could be.

I thank him so much for his energy, enthusiasm, support, great conversations, memories of Richard, an ability to keep a timeline in order, his relentlessness in keeping Richard on track . . . his boundless desire to see this story told well. Thanks Father.

Michael Donaldson
April 2019

ABOUT THE AUTHOR

Michael Donaldson is an Auckland-based freelance writer and editor. A former sports editor and deputy editor at the *Sunday Star-Times*, he has been a journalist for 30 years, specialising in sport and more recently beer . . . that is, pretty much the dream job. He is the editor of a specialist beer magazine, *The Pursuit of Hoppiness*, contributes to *DrinksBiz* magazine, and his beer writing is regularly published in *North & South*, the *New Zealand Herald* and *Stuff*. He blogs about beer at www.beernation.co.nz.

Michael's previous books include *Beer Nation: The Art and Heart of Kiwi Beer*, *The Big Book of Home Brew: A Kiwi Guide*, *Lydia Ko: Portrait of a Teen Golfing Sensation*, and he was co-author of Steve Williams' autobiography *Out of the Rough*.

Photo courtesy Rebekah Robinson/*North & South*.

For information on our other titles, visit:
www.penguin.co.nz